An Inconvenient Truth

An Inconvenient Truth

Crime, Religion, and Personal Responsibility

Ashley E. Davis

Foreword by Jason K. Davis

WIPF & STOCK • Eugene, Oregon

AN INCONVENIENT TRUTH
Crime, Religion, and Personal Responsibility

Copyright © 2025 Ashley E. Davis. All rights reserved. Except for brief quotations in critical publications or reviews, no part of this book may be reproduced in any manner without prior written permission from the publisher. Write: Permissions, Wipf and Stock Publishers, 199 W. 8th Ave., Suite 3, Eugene, OR 97401.

Wipf & Stock
An Imprint of Wipf and Stock Publishers
199 W. 8th Ave., Suite 3
Eugene, OR 97401

www.wipfandstock.com

PAPERBACK ISBN: 979-8-3852-3343-4
HARDCOVER ISBN: 979-8-3852-3344-1
EBOOK ISBN: 979-8-3852-3345-8

VERSION NUMBER 01/09/25

Unless otherwise noted, Scripture quotations are taken from the New King James Version. Copyright © 1982 by Thomas Nelson, Inc. All rights reserved. Used by permission.

Where noted, Scripture quotations are from The Holy Bible, Berean Standard Bible. BSB is produced in cooperation with Bible Hub, Discovery Bible, OpenBible.com, and the Berean Bible Translation Committee. This text of God's Word has been dedicated to the public domain.

FROM ASHLEY

For my children, Isaiah and Hadassah.
May you always follow your dreams
and be authentic to yourself. I love you both.

For my friend, Norman.
Thank you for all the thought-provoking
conversations at the fire station.

For Winston and Cleo,
Who are far better people than I am,
even though they are cats.

For my mother, Eve.
I love you higher than the heavens.

And for my husband, Jason.
I'd choose *you* 1,000 times over. Forever and always, my love.

FROM JASON

For Paisley.
Always follow your dreams.

Contents

Foreword by Jason K. Davis | ix
Abbreviations | xi

Chapter One: Introduction | 1

Chapter Two: Religious Roots of Crime | 14

Chapter Three: Crime in Antiquity | 25

Chapter Four: Modern Crime | 36

Chapter Five: The Officer—His Duty and Ethics | 56

Chapter Six: Conclusion | 69

Bibliography | 83

Foreword

FOR THE BETTER PART of the last twenty-six years, I have served as a deputy sheriff in a small, country town. I've seen and interacted with the comings and goings of those who go about their days and those who go about their travels, and I've also dealt with my fair share of criminals. Throughout the years, I've heard pretty much every excuse one can give for why they committed a crime. But very seldom has that excuse been the *real* reason they committed the crime—the selfishness of man—few have ever owned up to their personal culpability. Many, if not all, criminals I've arrested have flat out denied their involvement in the crime or have even gone so far as to say, "The devil made me do it." And, as time draws on, those excuses become ever more extravagant as people try to excuse their actions in the hopes that whatever façade they've been putting on, or whatever façade has overtaken their mind, becomes a reality.

As a law enforcement officer, it is hard to reconcile the fact that people cannot own up to their own crimes. No one has forced them to commit that crime; it was done purely out of their own free will. While some may argue against that notion, my knowledge,

FOREWORD

training, and experience as a deputy all these years have served to solidify my position.

As you'll see throughout the book, my wife (the author of this book) and I note that crime always contains an element of self-satisfaction. I believe that if one truly held to the morals that God has inscribed on the conscience of every man and woman, then they would take responsibility for their actions, in both the good choices and the bad.

Senior Deputy, Sgt. Jason K. Davis[1]

---

1. Jason K. Davis has served as both a deputy sheriff and a firefighter for the past twenty-six years. He currently holds the rank of sergeant at the sheriff's office and the rank of lieutenant at the fire department. This is his first book contribution.

Abbreviations

ANE	Ancient Near East
APA	American Psychological Association
HL	Hittite Laws
JSOTSupp	Journal for the Study of the Old Testament Supplement
LE	Laws of Eshnunna
LH	Laws of Hammurabi
LL	Lipit-Ishtar
MT	Masoretic Text
MAL	Middle Assyrian Laws

Chapter One

Introduction

Morality, like art, means drawing a line someplace.
—Oscar Wilde

THIS BOOK IS A story about *another* story, one that is as old as time. A story that has been prevalent from almost the beginning of creation. From the tantalizingly beautiful landscapes of a decidedly utopian world to the marred façade we walk so dimly through, Gen 3:1–7 recounts the story of when sin entered the world, and where sin has entered, crime has also reared its ugly head. The brutal truth of sin, that was ushered in through the garden of Eden, can be seen in the underlying lack of moral code that crime so often rests. The roots of crime are simple yet largely misunderstood. And it may be that it's less of a misunderstanding than the realization of personal culpability. The hard truth remains that crime, as I will argue, can only be chalked up to personal responsibility (not the "blame game") which has its roots in religion.

We live in a world that is said to be full of risk and danger. Every day, individuals are putting "themselves into positions where it becomes far more likely that they will offend. These actions constitute a continuum of conduct which range from putting oneself in a situation that makes offending virtually certain . . . to situations where the causal link is much weaker."[1]

The not-so-flattering character traits of greed and selfishness are the basis for why individuals decide to break the law. It is also my belief, along with many others, that there is ultimately no crime that does not contain an element of self-satisfaction. Read that statement again and take a moment to reflect on it. A break or lapse in moral character defines the rationale for most, if not all, of criminological activity. And in that criminological activity, there exists an element of self-satisfaction, whether it is to gain something tangible or gain some sort of emotional advantage (think: retaliation, etc.).

Throughout this book, we will define crime and make an attempt to understand its religious roots. After all, crime and religion go hand-in-hand. We will view the issue of personal responsibility through the lens of both a biblical and non-biblical perspective. Then, we will look at crime in antiquity through the modern age. It is important for law enforcement officers to understand these backgrounds in order to form their perspectives on not only how to deter crime but how to deal with it more effectively. Coping, or dealing with criminals and criminal activity, are only the tip of the iceberg. Theories in "redemptive criminology" have surfaced but most fall by the wayside, as the topics of redemption and forgiveness often appear marginal to the criminal justice system that is ostensibly "victim retribution focused."

Law enforcement is a field that takes a toll on its officers, no matter if they serve in a jail, on patrol, or in an investigative position. Thus, understanding crime from different perspectives allows these officers to contend with the moral obligations of such offenses and become more empathetic to the idea that personal responsibility starts with the criminal and ends with the criminal. This statement will be fleshed out throughout the book.

1. Dingwall and Hillier, *Blamestorming*, 115.

INTRODUCTION

DEFINING CRIME

"*Crime* may be defined as *an act of the breaking of a moral rule defined in criminal law*."[2] This may be the most basic definition of crime one can offer. The field of criminology is multi-faceted, whereby legal definitions of crime can include too much or too little information. With the integration of other disciplines into the field of criminology, the definitions and strategies then seemingly become all too complex. Sociology, the scientific and systematic study of human behavior, influences much of criminological ideology and thus the definitions of crime. One of the major influential factors is

> for some sociologists, crime must be a social construct, and it may be argued, can only be explained by other social constructs. Perhaps the best known representation of this view was made by Sutherland and Cressey, who admonished: "Although crime and criminality are by definition social phenomena, people have for centuries entertained the notion that they are products of non-social causes." (1978:118; see also Hirschi and Gottfredson 1980).[3]

Non-social causes of crime are essentially the *drive* behind criminal behavior. Enabling a personal culpability in criminological activity has both its benefits and limitations, and quite frankly the use of the term "crime," in and of itself, presents some semantic challenges.

Regardless, personal culpability remains at the forefront of the discussion. Crime has been portrayed as carefully thought-out schemes by well-trained individuals (think mafia-esque storylines like in the famous *Godfather* books and movies), when in fact it is quite the opposite. "Much, if not most criminal behaviour, is rather mundane, shortsighted, and seemingly adventitious. It produces little gain and engenders considerable long-term negative consequences for the actor. It tends not to be planned long in advance, but rather often seems nearly spontaneous (and, in

---

2. Wikström and Sampson, *Explanation of Crime*, 63 (italics in original quote).

3. Bosworth and Hoyle, *What Is Criminology?*, 38.

hindsight, even to the offender to be unaccountable)."[4] This very notion can be seen from the beginning of time, with the famous story of Cain and Abel.

Genesis 4 recounts the story of two brothers who brought offerings before God. A tale as old as time, Abel brought the first fruits of his flock as a sacrifice to the LORD while Cain brought only *some* of the best of his harvest, a theme interwoven throughout the pages of Scripture. When Cain saw that the LORD had shown favor to his brother, Cain flew into a jealous rage and murdered Abel. What, in the end, was the root cause of this crime that Cain had committed? He was jealous. He wanted something that his brother had (i.e., the LORD's favor) and thus decided that he was going to be selfish and "do away" with his brother in order to gain that favor. Remember when we mentioned that crime is always self-satisfying? It is not too far-fetched to argue that Cain viewed the murder of his brother in an advantageous light, *in the heat of the moment*, in order to gain prosperity when in fact all it did was cause him disparity. Cain's very name means "acquisition" in Hebrew, an inherently self-centered ideology. Hebrew names being reflective of one's character, Cain certainly emulated the qualities of greed and selfishness in his desire for acquiring what his brother possessed. Greed and selfishness in this story had reared their ugly heads, and their consequences were ultimately lifelong as Cain suffered through the production of evil descendants; and at the end of his decidedly miserable life, he died by the very instrument he used to kill his own brother.[5]

Crime is thus apparent from the beginning of time. Adam and Eve broke a moral rule in the garden of Eden in eating the fruit of the tree of knowledge of good and evil. Cain slew his brother Abel in a fit of rage, all to gain favor from God. Both of their actions were greed-filled and selfish in nature. Adam and Eve wanted

---

4. Bosworth and Hoyle, *What Is Criminology?*, 39.

5. The Bible is largely silent on the manner of Cain's death. Extrabiblical literature, as in the Book of Jubilees, suggests that Cain died by his house (which was made of stones) falling on top of him. Biblical accounts that Cain produced evil descendants, however, are prevalent throughout the Bible. His lineage is listed in Gen 4.

INTRODUCTION

to be like God. Cain wanted to be better than his brother Abel. In other words, each of these examples shows that crime is always for some sort of personal satisfaction; for Adam and Eve it was to gain knowledge, and for Cain it was to gain status. Crime is still committed for these reasons today, yet with a plethora of more options.

The bottom line is that each individual is endowed with a moral code and moral character. Whether one believes in God or not, there exists a consciousness about what is right and what is wrong. Much of greed and selfishness can be traced back to a sin problem, a problem that all of us struggle with on a daily basis. And when the struggle becomes all too heavy to bear, some individuals result to breaking the moral code in favor of using others as a personal crutch, a personal scapegoat for their moral culpability and moral responsibility to do the right thing.

It is evident from antiquity that crime and punishment were meted out through the avenues of justice, even though those avenues have changed considerably over millennia. And while it may seem overly simplistic, crime began at the start of it all . . . in the garden of Eden.

DEFINING SIN

Sin, by its very nature, is an inward, inherent condition—a controlling power that misguides its victim. Humans, by our very nature, are inclined to sin (make bad choices that are contrary to God's guidelines for our lives). Some predisposing factors of sin are ignorance, error, inattention, rebellion, and lack of integrity. Sin can be defined as *any failure to conform to the moral law of God in act, attitude, or nature*,[6] and sin is ultimately the direct result of Adam's fall through which good things have become corrupt (Gen 3:6).

Sin lies at the very crux of our hearts, where our decisions are made, and actions are born out of those decisions. Sin was introduced in the form of a question (Satan's method of getting Eve to doubt God's word). We find this starting in Gen 3:1. I personally

---

6. Allison, *Historical Theology*, 342.

believe that our hearts were predisposed to a sin nature because God, in his omniscience, knew what he had to do for us even before the creation of the world. This wasn't his intent (it certainly isn't from him—Jas 1:13), but he allowed it to happen in order to accomplish a purpose. In other words, it is solely the result of human actions (Jas 1:14–15).

When we read through the first few chapters of Genesis, we can readily see the effects of sin upon human nature and nature itself. Here is a list of the effects of sin:

- Genesis 3:7—sin distorts nakedness
- Genesis 3:13—this shows an inherent denial of sins, placing blame elsewhere
- Genesis 3:16—human desire is for authority or power
- Genesis 3:17–19—all of creation was cursed (human nature, nature itself)

The nature of sin manifests itself in actions like sensuality (works of the flesh: Gal 5:19–21), selfishness, and displacement of God (the Ten Commandments warn against this in Exod 20:3, as well as other passages like Mark 12:30). These actions show themselves in the desire to enjoy things, obtain things, and achieve things. Humans wrongly put *things* above God. We should note that those whose ways are wicked, they will perish apart from God (Ps 1:6).

Pelagius, the famed British monk and theologian (ca. AD 354–418), believed that whereas God had given human beings the capacity to fulfill the commandments, both volition and action were strictly human faculties. He believed that God created all human beings with the power to act, but their actions depended upon their willingness to engage in such actions. Thus, people act out of a capacity given to them by the grace of God, but their will and action are not assisted by grace. Grace, Pelagius said, was God's work to assist the capacity to be able to do good.[7]

St. Augustine of Hippo (AD 354–430), a contemporary of Pelagius, believed that Pelagius's view on human nature minimized

---

7. Allison, *Historical Theology*, 348–49.

INTRODUCTION

the importance of God's grace. Augustine believed that pride was the beginning of sin (Ecclesiasticus 10:13). Pride is simply "undue exaltation" according to Augustine; this is when the soul abandons God and becomes an end in itself. Humanity then lost the freedom it once enjoyed. He advocated that since people have a free will, they usually use it to do evil rather than good—the complete opposite of Pelagius's position. Augustine maintained that both death (the punishment for sin) and the corruption of human nature are passed down from Adam. We see this fleshed out in the book of Genesis.

With freedom comes responsibility, and there are those who choose to do wrong anyway and don't care about the consequences. I believe that sin does play a part in how man exercises his freedoms because more often than not people will choose to do what feels good (sin) rather than what is right. But should we resign freedom to a deterministic, historical chain of events, in which we really exercise no freedom in our own lives? No. It is a reality that we choose things—one over the other—because we are the originators of our own actions. With freedom comes responsibility, and we must be careful to choose the right moral path. To summarize Thomas Aquinas, morals and moral virtues are the habits that allow each individual to control the passions and desires that have a tendency to lead the individual away from their "true good."[8] Much of the crime that is committed is born out of the freedom to choose, with most offenses being made in the name of self-satisfaction and denial of a moral and ethical code. The search for admissibility and personal culpability thus remains on the part of the criminals as they flow through the criminal justice system.

DEFINING ETHICS

Since crime and ethics are at the core of the discussion for this book, a definition of ethics (in particular, *Christian ethics*) must also be addressed. Ethics, at its core, is defined as what is morally

---

8. Paulson, *Sin and Evil*, 29.

right and wrong. Thus, the field of ethics can be understood as the philosophical study of morality; for example, *how to know* what is right and what is wrong.

There are two approaches to the study of morality—descriptive ethics (factual studies of moral attitudes and behaviors) and metaethics, which consists of two sub disciplines (emotivism and metaethical relativism). Metaethics is the branch of philosophy that analyzes the meaning of certain moral terms, and there are theories in this branch that are referred to as noncognitivist and cognitivist. Cognitivist theories depict moral statements as indicatives. Objectivist theories imply that moral statements convey information about moral acts themselves or the objects which are said to have value. In more layman's terms, properly understanding the question "Why should I be moral?" and the question "What rational justification can be given to me as to why it would be reasonable to adopt the moral point of view rather than some other point of view, say, an egotistic self-interested point of view . . .?" is based on ethical and moral rationale.

There are specific issues in applied ethics that are approached by all people at some point in their lives, and they are either seen through the background of ethical relativism or ethical absolutism. Both realms are highly intricate and can oftentimes seem overly complicated. There are four different views on relativism: (1) Descriptive relativism is the view that cultures have basic ethical differences, (2) normative relativism thinks that a person should follow his or her society's code and that societies differ in the content of their codes, (3) metaethical relativism says that the meanings of moral terms are themselves relative to culture, (4) combinatorial relativism combines an absolute, formal principle with a relative, material principle to yield a relative action guide. There are ethical skeptics who think that moral truths do not exist, and even if they did, no one would know what they are. Absolutists disagree with moral relativists and assert the existence of absolutes. A moral absolute has three different meanings: (1) it is objectively true, (2) it is exceptionless, and (3) it is a principle with the highest degree of incumbency. Absolutism seems to favor theism, and that is where we will continue the discussion on ethics.

Ethics and Its Contribution to Christianity

The distinctive contribution Christianity and religion make to the world of ethics is that "morality lies in its comprehension of the dimension of depth in life." "A religious morality is constrained by its sense of a dimension of depth to trace every force with which it deals to some ultimate origin and to relate every purpose to some ultimate end. It is concerned not only with immediate values and disvalues, but with the problem of good and evil, not only with immediate objectives, but with ultimate hopes."[9] Even in the midst of a world defined by religiously based moral and ethical values, those individuals who hold to secular worldviews still derive their actions from a religious base. In other words, "secular moral acts resolve the conflicts of interest and passion"[10] in an immediate context, within the constraints of the adage *everything in moderation*.

The subject of ethics is too vast to confine to the pages of one small book. And the field of ethics can be characterized as problematic, however, as it assumes people will take responsibility for their own actions. "In order to judge a person's behavior as morally right or wrong there is usually an assumption that their actions are freely chosen. The idea of free will is therefore central to ethical reasoning and judgment."[11] What can be said, from a generic perspective in Christianity, is that moral considerations "feature prominently in Israel's laws and are clearly evident in the denunciation of the prophets against their contemporaries; moreover, many of the narratives contained in the historical books raise profound ethical questions, and moral issues frequently occur in the sayings of the wise and in various passages of the Psalms."[12] The

---

9. Niebuhr, *Interpretation of Christian Ethics*, 13.
10. Niebuhr, *Interpretation of Christian Ethics*, 13.
11. Prenzler, *Ethics and Accountability in Criminal Justice*, 3.
12. Davies, "Moral Vision of the Hebrew Bible," 154.

concept of morality according to Christian tenets is framed against the backdrop of Judaism in which morality was the "knowledge of a divine code, emanating from an authority external to human reason," a code that one obeys out of "trust in the promises and fear of the judgments of the Divine Lawgiver."[13]

Christian ethics, in particular, deals with what is morally right and wrong for a Christian according to the Bible. Numerous ethical "systems" exist, yet only a biblical worldview can account for moral laws and reasoning that are rooted in Scripture. Worldview thus plays a major role in determining which ethical system one follows. The following can be said about Christian ethics: 1. **It is based on God's will.** It upholds a divine-command position, meaning that God wills what is right in accordance with his own moral attributes. 2. **It is absolute.** Since God's moral character does not change, moral obligations (ethics) that flow from his nature are absolute . . . meaning that they also do not change. 3. **It is based on God's revelation.** Ethics are revealed in nature by general revelation and revealed in Scripture by special revelation. 4. **It is prescriptive.** Christian ethics is prescribed by a moral God, therefore it is "prescriptive." And 5. **It is deontological** (i.e., Christian ethics is "duty-centered"). All of these ethical attributes are bound up in one or more of the following six key ethical systems:

---

13. Sidgwick, *Outlines of the History of Ethics*, 111.

INTRODUCTION

Ethical Systems	Beliefs
Antinomianism	There are no moral laws
Situationism	One absolute law
Generalism	Some general laws, no absolute laws
Unqualified absolutism	Many absolute laws that never conflict
Conflicting absolutism	Many absolute norms that sometimes conflict; we are obligated to do the lesser evil
Graded absolutism	Many absolute laws sometimes conflict; we are responsible for obeying the higher law

Each individual will adhere to one of the above ethical systems, which lets other individuals know where they stand on the morality scale. Ethics, however, will always fall into the realm of subjectivity, whether we like that concept or not. When it comes to criminal behavior, then, the "separation between moral goodness based on the dictates of reason, on the one hand, and moral goodness based on obedience to a divine command, on the other, enables the perplexing problem of whether God's commandments are good because they have an intrinsic conformity to some standard of goodness shared by God and humanity (i.e., reason), or simply because they are God's commandments."[14] It is thus impossible to escape ethical reasoning and ethical judgment in our lives, as individuals judge one another's behavior in moral and ethical terms on a daily basis,[15] a concept that is especially prevalent in the criminal justice system.

DEFINING THE REST

"In so far as it is impossible to live at all without presupposing a meaningful existence, the life of every person is religious, with the possible exception of the rare skeptic who is more devoted to the observation of life than to living it, and whose interest in detailed facts is more engrossing than his concern for ultimate meaning

---

14. Bauerschmidt, "Ethics and the Triune God," 7.
15. Prenzler, *Ethics and Accountability in Criminal Justice*, 3.

and coherence."[16] For those who hold in high regard a *higher power* (for the Christian: God; for the Jew: *Adonai/YHWH*), the idea of a personal relationship with a deity who is so deeply interested and involved in the believer's life gives them a sense of divine accountability. In this view, "the deity has expectations of the believer's morality, and the believer is aware of those expectations as explicated in Scripture."[17]

Abandoning the moral and ethical ideals that the Creator had instituted and put into the conscience of all mankind would be a betrayal of the One who gave us life. One can abandon religiosity, but one cannot abandon the underwritten ideology of good and evil that have been instituted from the beginning of creation. St. Augustine expounded on this ideology in that, as a result of Adam's disobedience to God, original sin resides in the soul and is an integral part of each person; they are wholly connected. "It is the same sin that, according to Thomas Aquinas, clouds human reason and leaves man at the mercy of passion and desires rather than reason."[18] Choice, however, cannot be chalked up solely to nature. Greek philosopher Aristotle (384–322 BC) said it best when he advocated that the individual was the sole arbiter of their own actions: "When the origin of the actions is in him, it is also up to him to do them, or not to do them."[19]

Gaetano Filangieri, Italian jurist and philosopher of the eighteenth century, was a firm believer in the laws of nature. While he was not necessarily a religious individual, Filangieri's work *Science of Legislation* noted that human happiness depended on the laws of nature and its underlying moral tones:

> No man can ignore his laws, because they are not the ambiguous results of the maxims of the moralists, nor of the sterile meditations of the philosophers, but the dictates of that principle of universal reason, of that moral sense of the heart, which the author of nature has recorded in

16. Niebuhr, *Interpretation of Christian Ethics*, 13.
17. Lindholm, "Judaism in the Context of Western Ethical Plurality," 301.
18. Normore and Fitch, *Leadership in Education*, 165.
19. Aristotle, *Nicomachean Ethics*, book 3.

INTRODUCTION

all the individuals of our species, as a living measure of justice and honesty, which speaks to all men in the same language, and prescribes at all times the same laws.[20]

Where ethics and morals fail, we find a sinful nature that ushers in a culture of crime. And as the calls for holding criminals morally culpable for their actions ring louder and louder in the ears of law enforcement personnel, we can only rest on the moral and ethical standards in which individuals were created and our country was founded. Implementing a culture of personal responsibility in the criminal seems like a daunting task, and it may never, truly, be fully accomplished, but paving a way for understanding where the criminal fails, *and why*, is a road worthy to be taken.

---

20. Filangieri, *Ciencia de la legislación* (trans. Rivera), 65.

Chapter Two

Religious Roots of Crime

The intent of man's heart is evil from his youth.
—Genesis 8:21

There remains a large discrepancy in the discourse of modern criminal justice, one that is rooted in the disciplines of psychology, sociology, and scientific objectivity. What these disciplines tend to avoid when it comes to understanding criminals and the criminal justice system is the religious roots from which crime derives. The central message of the Judeo-Christian biblical text on personal culpability in light of sin appears to modern criminal justice practitioners as a "cop-out."

The idea that personal responsibility is the basis of *all* crime (to both the criminal and the officer) should serve to stir the pot and stimulate discussion. The approach that crime is rooted in the sinfulness and selfishness we see from the very beginning of creation in Gen 3:1–7 should be the basis of criminal justice dealings. In other words, when we understand that all crime comes from a personal desire or the root of selfishness, we can begin to not only empathize with the criminals but also offer different perspectives on how to talk with and "educate" them when they've committed a crime. There does exist a responsibility to educate the criminal; law enforcement officers should take the position that they "are obliged, by natural law, to give them the taste for sound precepts and to orient them so as to acquire a habit of virtue which, like a second nature, will guide their wills toward the good."[1] Yes, this is an overly simplistic way to think about educating the criminal, but intervention avenues have been shown to revitalize the criminals if they are ready and willing.

"If we want a revolution in the practices of justice (and of course not everyone does as some people are satisfied with the totalizing structures therein) then individual workers connecting with other stakeholders (victims, criminals, communities) need to reflect and act on their own potential for resistance and change."[2] In large part, this requires criminal justice practitioners, as well as the criminals themselves, to overcome our socially learned complicity in violence and also overcome the learned thoughts, feelings, and behaviors that contribute to the passing off of culpability from the individual who committed the crime to someone else, a.k.a. "the blame game." In order to accomplish this, understanding desire and free will from both biblical and non-biblical perspectives is a necessary step.

DIFFERING VIEWS: PERSONAL RESPONSIBILITY FROM A BIBLICAL PERSPECTIVE

Is it possible to speak the name of God in criminological discourse and criminal justice practice? The answer to this question depends on a number of factors. However, the answer should include a biblical perspective on the matter. The issue of personal responsibility ultimately hearkens back to creation, as mentioned many times throughout the short course of this book. Many laws found

---

1. Masferrer, "Role of Nature," 105.
2. Pycroft and Bartollas, *Redemptive Criminology*, 3.

in the biblical arena can be categorized as religious crimes or delict crimes. Religious crimes (such as apostasy, blasphemy, idolatry, and divination), however "criminal" in nature, are not against another person per se, thus they do not serve to be categorized as civil crimes like delict crimes. Delict crimes, by definition, are those felonious activities that serve to inflict or incite harm against another person. Both types of crime are addressed in the biblical text, most often found in the Torah and dealt with in a religious manner instead of a criminal manner. For example, in Deut 21:1–9, a homicide has taken place. The aim of the passage is not to punish the perpetrator in a criminal manner but to absolve the sinful aspects of the crime.[3] From a biblical perspective, the authors of Scripture are trying to *right* the person's moral code and bring them face-to-face with God and their moral responsibility. In the example of Deut 21:1–9, the elders of the town wash their hands of any immoral act (i.e., the murder that has taken place) and offer up a sacrifice for the atonement of sins in the event that their own actions will purge them from the guilt of innocent blood having been shed.

Personal Responsibility in the Garden of Eden

When one thinks of the ideal world, the best society, a place of happiness, they often give a biblical response to the garden of Eden. Poets and philosophers often reference the garden as a place of solace and good; it was universally understood that God's intention for mankind was a life of harmony and content without malice.[4] In the ancient world, the great Jewish philosophers also viewed the garden in these ways; Maimonides and Nahmanides are two of the most well-known.

For Maimonides (AD 1138–1204) the garden of Eden was a place of purity and reason. "Before their sin, Adam and Eve lived entirely in accordance with their intellects. Their goal was

---

3. Peled, "Laws of Delict in the Hebrew Bible," 6.
4. Wood, *Kant's Ethical Theory*, 227–28.

true human happiness: intellectual contemplation, scientific knowledge."[5] Sin, then, obscured reason in the garden, according to Maimonides, and ushered in the pursuit of imaginary desires and irrationality.[6]

For Nahmanides (AD 1194–1270), a contemporary of Maimonides who commented often on the garden's "natural necessity,"[7] he ultimately viewed Adam and Eve's sin in the following way:

> Through their sin, Adam and Eve acquired free will, that is, the ability to choose between "doing evil or good to themselves and to others." Although the power of choice is a divine attribute (see Genesis 3:5 and 23), it is harmful to human beings, for it incites in us problematic desires and lust (*yeser ve-ta'avah*). Interpreting Ecclesiastes 7:29, "God made man upright [*yashar*], but they have sought out many inventions," Nahmanides taught that God created Adam and Eve "upright," but they forsook the "one straight path" and sought out "many inventions" according to their free choice [*behirah*].[8]

When it comes down to it, the garden of Eden story was about maintaining a proper balance between intellect and desire. Through the desire to know more or gain more, a lapse in moral code, then, begins to rear its ugly head. This lapse falls within the purview of what is considered *evil*. "Evil is always the assertion of some self-interest without regard to the whole."[9] That ideology can be seen in the desire to become more like God or to essentially make a name for *themselves*, such as in the instance of the Tower of Babel (Gen 11:1–9).

There is hope, however, as emulated by the biblical example of Noah and his faithfulness to God. After the days of temptation, greed, and moral decline, Noah built an altar to the LORD. The sacrifice of clean animals was a way to cleanse his and humanity's

---

5. Harvey, "Four Jewish Visions," 221.
6. Maimonides, *Guide of the Perplexed*, 2.33, 364.
7. Nahmanides, *Perush ha-Torah*, 36.
8. Harvey, "Four Jewish Visions," 222.
9. Niebuhr, *Children of Light*, 9–10.

slate. Genesis 8:21 notes, "When the LORD smelled the pleasing aroma, He said in His heart, 'Never again will I curse the ground because of man, even though every inclination of his heart is evil from his youth. And never again will I destroy all living creatures as I have done'" (BSB). God's promise not to destroy mankind with a global flood almost suggests a reduction in overall punishment, no matter what the crime. "When God contemplates the future of humanity—a perspective that is characteristic of the utilitarian approach—it seems futile to demonstrate clemency. What is the benefit of mitigation if the defendant will commit the same crime in the future? It is only due to God's mercy—not necessarily supported by a rational argument—that human beings would not be punished again with the severity of the flood."[10] Thus, it can be said that a person's disposition toward criminal behavior is not convincing enough to exempt them from punishment altogether. God's bent toward mercy only serves to reduce the *severity* of the punishment, not to abolish it completely.

Revisiting Cain and Abel

Jewish and Christian interpretations of the first sibling rivalry, and subsequently the first murder after creation, reach far and wide. The Targums (Jewish/Aramaic translations of the books of the Hebrew Bible), however, shed some interesting light on the brothers from a criminological and religious standpoint. While the "targumic genre combines literal renderings of the biblical text with additional material, the additions provide important insights into ancient Jewish biblical interpretation."[11] The Targums paint Cain as wanting to be everything that his brother is not, meaning that he is seen as ever-straying further and further from God as he questions the principles of justice and mercy by which Judaism believed God governed the world.[12] A covetous heart for what his

---

10. Gold and Applebaum, "Inclination to Evil," 168.
11. McNamara and Flesher, "Targum."
12. Bassler, "Cain and Abel in the Palestinian Targums," 61.

brother could offer the LORD and the resulting favoritism toward his brother Abel from their Creator created in Cain an acquisition mindset, just as his name suggests.

Believing there would be no recompense for his sin, backed up by his own statement in Gen 4:9 ("Am I my brother's keeper?"), he wielded his might and took his brother's life in a fit of greed and selfishness. "The murder is the climax to a life marked by evil deeds and wrong doctrine. Ultimately, the reason Cain killed Abel was because of their differing theological positions."[13] Cain's belief that there would be no recompense for his sin, ultimately, did not hold himself personally culpable for his brother's murder. Divine retribution, however, awaited Cain—being enacted almost immediately when God questioned Cain about his brother's whereabouts. Thus, we find here the second example in biblical history of God putting someone *on trial* to take personal responsibility for their sins. Ancient philosopher and historian Plato even recognized that Cain represents the beginning of voluntary sin:

> Why does He who knows all ask the fratricide, "Where is Abel, thy brother?" He wishes that man himself of his own will shall confess, in order that he may not pretend that all things seem to come about through necessity. For he who killed through necessity would confess that he acted unwillingly; for that which is not in our power is not to be blamed. But he who sins of his own free will denies it, for sinners are obliged to repent. Accordingly, he (Moses) inserts in all parts of his legislation that the Deity is not the cause of evil (Plato, QG 1.68).[14]

Philo, a contemporary of Plato, sought to show that of his own free will Cain murdered his brother. John Byron notes that "Philo's picture of Cain has expanded to further depict him as one who willingly sins and attempts to hide the fact from God."[15] Hiding the facts from an omniscient (all-knowing) Creator further serves to demonstrate that morality is inherent; we are all created with a

---

13. Byron, *Cain and Abel in Text and Tradition*, 69.
14. Byron, *Cain and Abel in Text and Tradition*, 83.
15. Byron, *Cain and Abel in Text and Tradition*, 83.

moral compass that serves as a guide to right and wrong and thus precipitates the need for personal responsibility for our actions.

Morality and Personal Responsibility

As you will see in the next chapter, legal provisions were apparent from antiquity. Provisions existed already in the Ten Commandments (Exod 20:2–14; Deut 5:6–18), but these were not *legal statutes* as found in the ancient manuscripts. These provisions were based solely on moral and ethical grounds, meaning that they should be viewed as moral and ethical directives as it relates to crime and the punishments for those crimes. Those moral and ethical directives likely were the basis for later biblical law collections.[16]

Much of Scripture even speaks on subjection to a constituted authority. Charles C. Ryrie notes:

> Angelic beings are subject to Christ (1 Peter 3:22); believers are to be subject to one another (1 Peter 5:5); the Church is subject to Christ (Eph. 5:24); the Son shall be subject to the Father (1 Cor. 15:28); servants are subject to their masters (1 Peter 2:18); children are under their parents (1 Tim. 3:4); wives are subject to their husbands (Col. 3:18); young people are to be subject to their elders (1 Peter 5:5); church members are to be governed by their leaders (Heb. 13:7, 17); and believers are to be subject to their government. It is a part of a total doctrine of obedience.[17]

The obedience that Ryrie speaks of can even be demonstrated in the garden of Eden with Adam and Eve. Initially, they were obedient and submissive to God. But when something crept in that challenged their morals and challenged their thinking, they gave in to disobedience.[18] While their actions were concertedly futile,

16. Frymer-Kensky, "Israel," 975–76.
17. Ryrie, "Christian and Civil Disobedience," 438.
18. There has been an argument that the sinful actions of mankind were due to the *creation* of Eve herself. Anderson and Oppong note that Adam initially had a good relationship with God, and Eve's creation just caused Adam strife, thus causing the ushering in of sinfulness and oppression. See Anderson and Oppong, "Wife Battery," 16–22.

in the ushering in of sin, actions of modern-day individuals do not have to play out in such a macabre way. Personal responsibility and the "righting of wrongs" can bring one to find solace amid a less contentious life, which rests on the judgment one might face before God (Rom 14:12).

DIFFERING VIEWS: PERSONAL RESPONSIBILITY FROM A NON-BIBLICAL PERSPECTIVE

Morality exists on a level of consciousness that is endowed by each individual, regardless of age, sex, or even religious affiliation. One of the issues that has plagued both ancient and modern times is civil disobedience. At the core, civil disobedience is a peaceful way to protest laws that the individual does not agree with (i.e., paying taxes); thus, it is based on the principles that regulate civil life.[19] The principle of civil disobedience maintains an underlying tenet of creation and the Judeo-Christian mindset. In other words, "in principle [civil disobedience] recognizes the prima facie claim of governmental authority, and in method it appeals to moral sympathy in the general populace. Civil disobedience seeks to bring law and morality into greater congruence, and this congruence underlies the respect for law."[20] It would seem, then, that law and morality go hand-in-hand. And where morality exists, rules must also exist, no matter what religious belief system one holds to.

In a world of conflicts, the "knowledge of good and evil seems to be the aim of all ethical reflection."[21] Ultimately, a nonbiblical perspective hinges on the auspices of classical and neoclassical thought. Both ideologies insist that human beings are fundamentally rational and most human behavior results from free will coupled with rational choice. The determining factors in human behavior stem from pain and pleasure; and it is sometimes necessary to forfeit some of the pleasures to form an orderly

---

19. Rawls, "Justification of Civil Disobedience," 247.
20. Zashin, *Civil Disobedience and Democracy*, 127.
21. Bonhoeffer, *Ethics*, 21.

society. Crime then, in essence, is a disruption of an orderly society. During the Enlightenment, free will became the forefront of discussion and "for the first time... free will and rational thought came to be recognized as the linchpins of all significant human activity. In effect, the Enlightenment inspired the reexamination of existing doctrines of human behavior from the point of view of rationalism."[22] Its views were akin to the argument of the current work, that personal responsibility and morality are at the core of criminological activity. Frank Schmalleger notes:

> Crime and deviance, which had previously been explained by reference to mythological influences and spiritual shortcomings, took their place in Enlightenment thought alongside other forms of human activity as products of the exercise of free will. Once people were seen as having control over their own lives, crime came to be explained as a particularly individualized form of evil—that is, as moral wrongdoing fed by personal choice.[23]

The prevalent view for much of antiquity, it wasn't until the 1800s that another school of thought was ushered in: positivism. The main underlying concept of the positivism movement was that crime resulted from forces outside of the individual (i.e., social status, culture, age, gender, etc.). Crime then, was not a result of personal choice or moral lapses in judgment but was a force enacted on the individual, thus placing the blame on other factors than the self. Personal responsibility had fallen by the wayside in non-religious contexts.[24]

For the secularist, the complex ways of life and religion owe their respects to the evolutionary processes that have shaped minds

---

22. Schmalleger, *Criminology Today*, 59.
23. Schmalleger, *Criminology Today*, 59.
24. While it is certainly true that one can look around them today and see that criminals, no matter if they ascribe to a religion or not, will blame others for their own choices and actions, there did exist some sort of accountability present in the historical viewpoints of personal responsibility. Jews and Christians viewed that they would be accountable before God for their actions (Rom 14:12), while those who did not ascribe to a particular religion believed that it is socially acceptable to blame their own actions on others.

over thousands of years in part due to cultural evolution. Most honest and perceptive secularists will (albeit hastily) admit that

> religion serves crucial functions in society. It helps to bind individuals into morally cohesive communities through ritual, it demarcates the normative boundaries of behaviour, and it provides a form of "supernatural" policing to promote cooperation, especially among co-religionists. In all of these ways, religion intertwines with the secular concerns of criminologists—crime, punishment, conflict, and the law.[25]

While religion is a subject that certainly divides opinions, it is a central feature of everyday life in that it can promote purpose and meaning that serves to enhance self-worth in those who do not commit crimes,[26] while also serving as a central facet (and subsequent fuel) of hate crimes, wars, and the like in those who choose the criminal life.[27] Regardless of living in a secular age, religion persists. And its persistence necessitates the need for personal culpability, not only in everyday life but in the criminal life as well. Paul Bloom is correct in his analysis as he argues, "It is impossible to make sense of most of human existence, including law, morality, war, and culture, without some appreciation of religion and how it works."[28]

"Religion," in the most basic sense, serves to promote a sense of belonging as individuals view themselves as members of groups who hold to the concept of community and tradition. In this vein, "specific religions can be viewed as forms of culture."[29] These collective values, norms, beliefs, and practices provide a source of social identity that "tends to bind individuals into particular types of community—moral communities—with specific rules about behaviors that are and are not permitted."[30] These *religious*

25. Durrant and Poppelwell, *Religion, Crime and Punishment*, 9.
26. Park, Edmondson, and Hale-Smith, "Why Religion?," 157.
27. Hitchens, *God Is Not Great*, 56.
28. Bloom, "Religion, Morality, Evolution," 181.
29. Cohen and Varnum, "Beyond East vs. West," 5–9.
30. Graham and Haidt, "Beyond Beliefs," 140–50.

communities can be defined by an adherence or non-adherence to a personal deity. Thus, both laws and *theology* (belief systems) function hand-in-hand.

The same sentiments are admonished by Mark Hill QC, in that he notes, "Several aspects of current criminal law are hard to understand without it [theology]."[31] Law and theology are unconvincing without showing respect to one another and ignoring their histories. Hill goes on to note, "The nature of both professions thus invites attention to basic questions of legal theory. It is natural for us to ask why certain acts deserve to be condemned and punished while other apparently similar acts do not, and religion always requires thinking seriously about the basic problems of right and wrong."[32] Thus, regardless of religious affiliation, the problems of right and wrong arise from a moral code inscribed on the conscience of all men and women. The need for personal culpability still stands at the forefront of the issue, regardless of the presence or absence of a personal deity.

---

31. Hill, "Introduction," 5.
32. Hill, "Introduction," 5.

Chapter Three

Crime in Antiquity

When reason fails, the devil helps.

—Dostoevsky (from *Crime and Punishment*)

THE BIBLE IS A text that very rarely conceals truths, and I say *rarely* because this is a largely debated point in biblical scholarship. If one contends that a proper hermeneutic for exegeting the text exists, then hard truths are apparent in the biblical text from the very beginning. Modern scholarship *may* have intended to conceal these truths, but the texts from antiquity are overwhelmingly assured of themselves when it comes to speaking of the cycle of sin, judgment, and redemption (all of which exist, in some part, in the modern criminal justice system). While crime figures prominently throughout the books of the New Testament (e.g., in the parables) as a veritable gallery of rogues make their entrance onto the grand scene, much of the law governing these crimes and criminals was formulated by criminal activity in the ancient Near East. Thus the reason for a short review of ancient Near Eastern biblical law and the study of selected Old Testament texts in this chapter.

AN INCONVENIENT TRUTH

Ancient Near Eastern and biblical law is somewhat of a captivating subject. When one thinks of the Bible, they don't automatically think of crime. However, manuscripts from antiquity record law-related events and customs of the ancient Israelites as well as their contemporaries—the Babylonians, Sumerians, Assyrians, and Hittites.[1] While there is no doubt that biblical law of the ancient Israelites borrowed from other contemporary cultures, their writings also stand as a monument to modern, Western law. The foremost authority on ancient Near Eastern and biblical law, Raymond Westbrook, notes, "The ancient Near East also has the distinction of being the cradle of the two great modern Western legal systems, the Common Law and the Civil Law, and in consequence of modern law in general."[2]

Of the manuscripts discovered from antiquity, the law collections contain over 300 statutes that address crimes that would be considered felonies. Five categories of felonies exist in the ancient Near Eastern manuscripts: theft (126 statutes), damage (91 statutes), homicide (40 statutes), injury (39 statutes), and a category that combines perjury, insult, slander, and false accusations (18 statutes).[3] Punishment for these felonious activities included the death penalty; yet, the death penalty is rarely mentioned outside the Torah, and capital punishment is rarely mentioned throughout Hebrew Scripture with the exception of a few times in the Prophets and Writings. In fact, "death was the penalty over 40 times and for more than 20 offenses in the Pentateuch (Brugger 2014, p. 60), including profaning the Sabbath (Exod 31:14), striking or cursing either of one's parents (Exod 21:15, 17; Lev 20:9), adultery (Lev 20:10; Deut 22:22), and blasphemy (Lev 24:16)."[4]

---

1. Westbrook, "Introduction," 8–10; Roth, *Law Collections from Mesopotamia and Asia Minor*, 1–10.
2. Westbrook, "Introduction," 1n1.
3. Peled, "Laws of Delict in the Hebrew Bible," 3.
4. Winright, "Crucifixion, Torture, and Capital Punishment," 264.

THE TORAH'S INFLUENCE ON WESTERN JURISPRUDENCE

Jurisprudence is the theory, or philosophy, of law. It has oftentimes been referred to as the *science of law*, which has its roots in the Roman period. What is oftentimes overlooked, however, is how Western (American) jurisprudence hearkens back to the biblical era as the Torah lays the foundation for much of our legal system today. The influence of the Torah not only goes above and beyond how laws are formed and enforced but advocates for the equality of all men and women. "The idea that it takes more than the word of one to prove that a person is guilty of a crime and that everyone is responsible for his or her actions alone, is derived from the Torah."[5] This is exemplified in Deut 19:15, which states, "A single witness shall not suffice to convict a person of any crime of wrongdoing in connection with any offense that may be committed. Only on the evidence of two or three witnesses shall a charge be established."

Personal responsibility is thus based on the moral codes emphasized in the Torah, which draws forth the reality of personal culpability in the stories the Torah tells that unfold surrounding criminal procedure . . . especially in the Ten Commandments. "Where the laws tell, the stories show, for example the wrath of God with the banishment from Eden, and God's mercy when Lot is spared from the destruction of Sodom and Gomorrah. Each tale gives strength to a different aspect of the laws."[6] Western jurisprudence has established that even though there is equality regarding moral codes and culpability, the idea of equal does not necessarily mean the same. The biblical example of Lot and Sodom and Gomorrah shows that he was faithful and righteous among a wicked and rebellious population. Lot was not punished for living among the people of Sodom and Gomorrah, even though it may have not been the wisest move to live there; he was not "guilty by association." What this does show, however, is the idea of *innocent until proven guilty*. Genesis 18:20–21 says, "Then the LORD said, 'The

---

5. Stanberry, "Western Jurisprudence," 316.
6. Stanberry, "Western Jurisprudence," 315.

outcry against Sodom and Gomorrah is great. Because their sin is so grievous, I will go down to see if their actions fully justify the outcry that has reached me. If not, I will find out.'" The idea here that espouses *innocent until proven guilty* frames modern Western jurisprudence; it serves as the backbone of our laws and punishment. These laws, rooted in the Torah, are the guide to life and action, no matter what one chooses, good or bad.

BIBLICAL EXAMPLES FROM ANTIQUITY

The Code of Hammurabi is said to have exerted a tremendous influence on Hebrew law. But the first five books of the Hebrew Bible, especially the Ten Commandments found in the book of Exodus, are credited with "providing the foundation for legal systems throughout much of the Western World."[7] More of a sympathetic form of punishment, Hebrew punishment inflicted on the aggressor was the same as the victim's suffering. Mitchel Roth notes:

> No adage is more prominent in the annals of crime and punishment as "an eye for an eye, a life for a life." This very literal view of accountability can be found in Exodus 21:23, where it is stated: "Life for life, eye for eye, tooth for tooth, hand for hand, foot for foot, burning for burning, wound for wound, stripe for stripe." It was only in post-biblical times that commentators began to interpret these words allegorically, as setting a limit to punishment, as in "up to an eye" or "up to a tooth."[8]

Criminal codes and punishments such as noted in the quote above can be found all throughout the Torah. This *lex talionis* code in Exod 21:1—23:33 has been identified as a legal text and has been called "the Book of the Covenant" or "the Covenant Code," based on Exod 24:7. Most of the statues pertaining to civil and criminal matters are found here and in the "Deuteronomic Code" in Deut 12–26. There also exists a "Holiness Code" in the book of Leviticus

---

7. Roth, *Eye for an Eye*, 29.
8. Roth, *Eye for an Eye*, 30.

(12–26), which is geared more toward proper action in the Levitical priesthood than it is to the regular members of ancient society. The *continuity* of criminal punishment, notably, is found throughout the Torah (the first five books of the Hebrew Bible) and, as mentioned previously, lays the foundation for Western jurisprudence. Many examples from biblical antiquity exist, so we will look at a few in the following sections.

TRIAL SCENES IN BIBLICAL ANTIQUITY

Modern categories such as criminal and civil law are implied throughout much of the biblical criminal accounts. Civil laws are usually termed under agreements between people for property (called contracts or torts), inheritance, and harm that involves some sort of compensation. The more criminal biblical accounts define acts that harm others, specifically by putting others at risk while there is no real way of compensating with time or money to the victim or their family. Criminal intent, both now and in biblical times, involves the offender's intent to cause harm (i.e., that lapse in moral code we've been going on and on about), resulting in a criminal trial.

One of the first "trial" scenes in biblical antiquity can be found in Gen 38:24–25 with Tamar and Judah. While this may not seem very "criminal" in nature, prostitution was considered a capital offense in the modern sense, thus inciting a trial in the case of Tamar's pregnancy. Genesis 38:24–25 says,

> And it came to pass, about three months after, that Judah was told, saying, "Tamar your daughter-in-law has played the harlot; furthermore she is with child by harlotry." So Judah said, "Bring her out and let her be burned!" When she was brought out, she sent to her father-in-law, saying, "By the man to whom these belong, I am with child." And she said, "Please determine whose these are—the signet and cord, and staff."

Judah, by way of his kinship, was a responsible party in the crime of prostitution. Tamar *did*, in fact, play the harlot . . . committing a capital offense of prostitution, but Judah was a co-conspirator in the matter. Tamar eventually was "let off the hook," as Judah did take the blame for getting her pregnant with his child. Although there is no explicit mention of a trial in the biblical account, Tamar did, in fact, have the chance to speak on her behalf. She produced "critical evidence" in the case by supplying Judah's signet, cord, and staff, thus exonerating her from the punishment of prostitution. It would be reasonable to assume that the evidence she had presented at the trial is what secured her "win" in the case.

Another famous "trial scene" in antiquity involved the king of the land, David himself. As David committed adultery with Bathsheba, his morality seemingly kicked in *after* the rendezvous and he tried to cover up his infidelity by tricking her husband, Uriah, into sleeping with her. When that didn't work, David arranged to kill Bathsheba's husband, Uriah, in battle. A morally repugnant action by the man whom YHWH himself instituted as king over Israel and Judah, this couldn't be left unpunished. The trial ends up being between YHWH and David, through the questions presented by Nathan the prophet. Nathan approached David in a judicial capacity and told him a story about a rich man and a poor man, whereby the rich man stole from the poor man, killed his lamb, and served it to his guests for dinner (2 Sam 12:1–4). The subsequent verses (5–7) note David's response to the dilemma:

> So David's anger was greatly aroused against the man, and he said to Nathan, "As the Lord lives, the man who has done this shall surely die! And he shall restore fourfold for the lamb, because he did this thing and because he had no pity." Then Nathan said to David, "You are the man! Thus says the Lord God of Israel: 'I anointed you king over Israel, and I delivered you from the hand of Saul.'"

In David's infinite wisdom, he would have had the man pay restitution, thus he ordered himself to pay a fourfold restitution according to the guidelines set out in Exod 21:37 (cf. Hebrew MT). In this trial scene, David essentially induced moral culpability upon himself as he recognized the error of his ways and was morally and ethically wrong. While some may argue that David should have been penalized more than he was, it would be safe to say that YHWH used this as an object lesson in ethics and morality that served its purpose in antiquity through the modern age.

Trials in antiquity (and it can be argued that they serve the same purpose in modernity) are an act of establishment and formal response to societal concerns "for predictability and trustworthiness in the aftermath of a criminal event by establishing and reaffirming the social norms and values that are deemed necessary to maintain stability and cohesion."[9] The trial "demonstrates to whatever audience is concerned where the line is drawn between behavior that belongs in the special universe of the group and behavior that does not."[10] In other words, it serves to shed a negative light on the offender, thus making him an outcast of the community.

LAW CODES FROM CONTEMPORARY CULTURES IN THE ANE

Other Near Eastern collections, contemporary cultures with the Israelites, contain legal material. The collections are written in cuneiform text and referred to as Laws of Ur-Namma, Laws of Lipit-Ishtar (LL), Laws of Eshnunna (LE), Laws of Hammurabi (LH), Hittite Laws (HL), Middle Assyrian Laws (MAL), and Neo-Babylonian Laws. The chart below lists some of the codes found in the contemporary legal code along with their biblical references. Most biblical references come from the Covenant Code and the Deuteronomic Code.

---

9. Pointer, *Restorative Justice Ritual*, 38.
10. Erikson, *Wayward Puritans*, 11.

Code Enforced[11]	Biblical Reference(s)	Contemporary Reference(s)
Debt slavery	Exod 21:2–6; Deut 15:12–16	LH §117
Injuries to the person resulting in compensation	Exod 21:18–19	LH §206; HL §10
Women who have been assaulted and miscarry a child	Exod 21:22–25	LL §25; LH §§209–14; HL §17; MAL A §§50–51
Requirement that rapists must marry the woman they raped	Exod 22:15–16; Deut 22:28–29	MAL A §§55–56
Talionic punishment for false accusers	Deut 19:16–21	LL §17; LH §§1–4
Goring of one bull by another	Exod 21:35	LE §53

These are just a handful of the legal codes that were enforced among biblical and contemporary cultures in the ancient Near East. The codes' influence among the ancient Mesopotamian region, although varied, arguably demonstrates that there were some normative and religious foundations of modern law in Mesopotamian culture. Without regard to religious contexts, most (if not all) criminal laws in the ancient Near East espoused a humane spirit, a theme that is woven throughout the pages of the Torah, espousing purity and ethical fruitfulness.[12] "Life within the[se] communities [were] regulated by laws based on moral concepts of right and wrong; the breaking of these laws met with severe punishment."[13] Mesopotamian culture highly regarded piety, and those who were offenders in the ancient Near East would be at the mercy of the gods, eliciting divine anger as a punishment for neglecting their cultic duties.[14] In other words, piety and morality played a role in

11. Strawn, "Biblical Law."

12. Wiedemann, "Moses or Hammurabi?," 108. See also Oettli, *Gesetz Hammurabis und die Thora Israels*, 87.

13. Brooks, *Contribution to the Study of the Moral Practices*, 89.

14. Oshima, "Morality and the Minds of the Gods," 401.

ancient Mesopotamian culture when it came to carrying out the divine mandate to advance justice and enhance quality of life.

CRIMINAL EXAMPLES FROM PHARAONIC EGYPT

In a short, but compelling, article by Renate Müller-Wollermann about crime in Pharaonic Egypt, we learn there were only two types of crime: crimes against the state and crimes against the person. Crimes against the state included treason, *lèse majesté*, and desertion. Crimes against the person included the felonies we are all too familiar with in our own society: murder, bodily injuries, adultery, rape, and theft. Unfortunately, there is scant evidence from the Egyptian manuscripts regarding the punishments for said crimes. However, archaeological evidence suggests that death penalties did indeed play out in ancient Egypt. Müller-Wollermann notes, "Mummies and skeletons also provide some evidence for killings and even murder. A skeleton of a woman in Abydos reveals that she was stabbed in the back with a blade, that even hit her ribs around the front of the thorax. A mummy head found in Thebes shows that the man was struck dead with an instrument when he was lying down sleeping or was unconscious."[15] This demonstrates what we find in the ancient Egyptian Edfu texts (texts that date to the Ptolemaic period, roughly 305–30 BC, which describe various myths and legends of that period), especially in the "Myth of the Sun's Eye" that describes a *lex talionis* ("eye for an eye") type of justice.[16]

What we find in ancient Near Eastern texts is that biblical and non-biblical law both have a tendency to discriminate between the seriousness of the offenses and the seriousness of committing the same offense, but in different ways.[17] The judgments in each individual case also involve a high degree of moral evaluation. The

---

15. Müller-Wollermann, "Crime and Punishment in Pharaonic Egypt," 229. Müller-Wollermann cites Baker, "Contributions of Biological Anthropology," 111.

16. Ritner, *Libyan Anarchy*, 129.

17. Burnside, *Signs of Sin*, 225.

punishments, then, are in relation to the moral culpability of the crime committed.

INTERPRETING BIBLICAL CRIME IN THE MODERN AGE

Moral code and character are often topics among biblical accounts of crime. In later centuries, concern for law, crime, and morality were the topics of some of the greatest Christian thinkers. Crime and its moral counterpart were treated with the utmost care and concern in the works of St. Augustine, Thomas Aquinas, Martin Luther, John Calvin, and other famous Christian theologians. Despite the modern institutions of *nemo tenetur prodere se ipsum* (no one is bound to betray himself) and *mens rea* (the intent of knowledge of wrongdoing on the criminal's part in the commission of a crime), their connection to Christianity often goes unrecognized.

When it comes to the modern age, however, morality and personal culpability only seem to play a small part as well. Punishment is meted out through differing avenues in the biblical world, just as it is meted out in modern-day justice. Some have argued that modern-day punishments have no effect on the criminal, but I would argue that punishment is symbolic of an internal struggle, whereby it serves to symbolize the struggle of corruption the criminal acts upon. This is an ideology that Christopher D. Marshall advocated for: "Punishment *symbolizes the corrupting impact of the misdeed on the wrongdoer's own person.*"[18] His ideology is based on the *theology* of Walter Moberly's "inverse sacraments." Inverse sacraments in the realm of crime and punishment are meant to provide some sort of retributive justice to the criminal and promote moral restoration. In a sense, it is reminiscent of penitential punishment, a term used to describe the "amendment of character, or conversion—that halts the moral debilitation that accompanies wrongdoing."[19] Moberly quite astutely noted:

---

18. Marshall, *Beyond Retribution*, 137 (italics in original quote).
19. Marshall, *Beyond Retribution*, 138.

> In punishment, the individual wrongdoer is himself an object of attention. His own pain and humiliation are partly designed to bring home to him symbolically the real nature of his deed, both its moral damage to himself and its calamitous repercussions on others. . . . His punishment is intended to induce him to rue his deed and to be ashamed of himself. If it is to fulfil this purpose, penal pain must ultimately be transmuted into penitential pain.[20]

No punishment itself can annul or atone for the crime committed; it serves as a symbolic act of restorative justice. The only true annulment gained through the punishment of criminological activity is the personal culpability of the offender; that is, "the reformation of the offender . . . the healing of the victim and the restoration of the damaged relationships to wholeness,"[21] an ideology that is wholly foundational to the relational and redemptive aspects of Christianity.

---

20. Moberly, *Ethics of Punishment*, 221.
21. Marshall, *Beyond Retribution*, 138.

Chapter Four

Modern Crime

The source of every crime is some defect of the understanding; or some error in reasoning; or some sudden force of the passions.

—Thomas Hobbes

INDIVIDUAL AND ORGANIZED CRIME is spreading like a global virus. Reputations for violence depend on long-term relations, which are traditionally cemented in long-term independent networks of friendship, kinship, and ethnicity.[1] These networks form an ontological database of crime. Ontology is the "branch of metaphysics dealing with the nature of being."[2] In more basic terms, it is the study of "what there is, what exists, what the stuff of reality is made out of, [and] secondly, what the most general features and relations of these things are."[3] Basically, it is the understanding of where everything comes from and why it is that way. We touched on ontology briefly, from a religious standpoint, as moral character

1. Varese, *Mafias on the Move*, 4.
2. *Merriam Webster Dictionary*, "Ontology."
3. Hofweber, "Logic and Ontology."

flowed from the garden of Eden and the creation context. However, with the advent of scientific discovery and the ushering in of positivism (the theory in criminology that is used to explain and predict criminal behavior), modern crime has developed a decidedly different bent than crime in antiquity as it relates to ethics and personal responsibility.

MODERN CRIME: A BACKGROUND

Any criminology student who picks up a textbook will find that the history of modern crime will begin with its founding fathers: Quetelet, Beccaria, Bentham, Lombroso, and W. E. B. DuBois, whose works were published throughout the eighteenth and nineteenth centuries.[4] The "founding fathers'" works were born out of ideologies relating sin and criminal nature from the seventeenth century as you will see as in the brief overviews that follow. Each of their contributions were based on different facets of the criminal justice system, yet they all contain a similar element—blame. Adolphe Quetelet (1796–1874), an astronomer and statistician, viewed crime as a social phenomenon whereby it (crime) could be calculated using statistical methods and sociological constructs. His philosophical representation of *l'homme moyen* (the average man) embodied all the qualities of the perfect individual, both physical and moral.[5] Over time, nationality, race, and other social factors began to influence *l'homme moyen*'s tendency for criminological activity.[6]

Cesare Beccaria (1738–94), on the other hand, focused on the punishments for such crimes and believed more wholeheartedly in retribution and not retaliation. His insistence on punishments that

---

4. Dooley and Rocque, "Criminology's Future Is in Its Past." Criminal nature and sin were touched on before the eighteenth and nineteenth centuries, in the seventeenth century, by some of the founding fathers and foreign philosophers and jurists.

5. Quetelet, *Système social*.

6. See the following reference (in French): Halbwachs, *Théorie de l'homme moyen*.

fit the crime (along the lines of the biblical *lex talionis*) ushered in a new way of thinking, and his principles were widely accepted in the French penal code of 1791. Beccaria, who was a devout Catholic, was one of the "founding fathers" who still believed that criminals had control over their own behavior and *chose* to participate in the commission of crimes.[7]

Jeremy Bentham (1748–1832), a contemporary of Beccaria, placed much emphasis on the pain versus pleasure aspect regarding criminological behavior. Subtle undertones of Bentham's work suggested that criminals weigh crime on a moral scale but also weigh the punishment. In other words, criminals weigh the benefits the crime can bring them and the pain that punishment from the commission of that crime can bring. Bentham was undoubtedly influenced not by religion but by nature, and believed that Nature was the purveyor of pain and pleasure.[8] In essence, Bentham was a hedonist (someone who believes that the pursuit of pleasure is the most important thing in life). Crime, then, could be measured on a scale of what type of pleasure it brought without regard to the true crime of morality and ethics.

Lombroso (1835–1909) might have advanced the most interesting stance on criminology of all the founding fathers, that crime was completely biological. Only after biological influence were social factors, well, a factor. Charles A. Ellwood, writing on Lombroso's theory, noted:

> The main or central position in Lombroso's theory, which was that crime is primarily due to biological or organic conditions. In other words, Lombroso's theory of crime was a completely biological theory, into which, especially in the later years of his life, he attempted to incorporate the social and psychological factors which are also manifestly concerned in production of crime. Lombroso believed, in other words, that the criminal was essentially an organic anomaly, partly pathological and partly atavistic. The social causes of crime were at most, according to Lombroso,

---

7. Beccaria, *Essay on Crimes and Punishments*.
8. Bentham, *Introduction to the Principles of Morals and Legislation*.

simply the stimuli which called forth the organic and psychical abnormalities of the individual.[9]

Lombroso's view of degenerate heredity had directed the path for the last "founding father," W. E. B. DuBois (1868–1963). W. E. B. DuBois's activism in the African American crime movement sought to advance the theory of social pressures in black communities. DuBois thought that black crime was not due to their natural genetic makeup but was a direct result of the "degradation and social disruption caused by slavery."[10] In other words, a biological condition of darker skin caused the oppression, which in turn triggered the criminological behavior.

Other than Beccaria, the modern founding fathers of criminology all posited outside sources as the cause and drive of criminal activity. They each pursued avenues of study that, in turn, had a major effect in demeaning personal culpability (and also inherent personhood), thus placing it in the hands of fate. These avenues also paved the way for the integration of more scientific studies on crime, ushering in a more complex network of personal scapegoats.

SCIENTIFIC SEGUES

It has been said that the genetic makeup of an individual determines whether or not they will commit a crime. I think this is a load of garbage, and let me tell you why, as I dip into the more colloquial side of this book, and the sciences in general. I've studied microbiology for the better part of ten years, working diligently in a lab examining both plant and animal genetics . . . usually hands deep in commensal and pathogenic bacteria. I wanted to understand how genes work and how we can manipulate them to do what we want them to do (think of the whole desired traits ordeal).

The entirely ironic underpinning of any scientific endeavor is the realization that a Creator is apparent down to the smallest of microbes, the smallest of atoms, and the smallest of genes. The irony

---

9. Ellwood, "Lombroso's Theory of Crime," 717.
10. Gabbidon, "W.E.B. DuBois on Crime," 3.

lies in the simple fact that genes can turn themselves on and off, almost like a light switch in the presence of certain environmental conditions within the body. This is called *gene transcription and regulation*. Cells are specialized within the body and the proteins, along with DNA, code for regulation of the brain, liver, pancreas, etc. . . . you get the idea. In the presence of stressors or changes in environmental conditions of the gut or other underlying negative influences, these genes can control what they do and when they do it. Their response is akin to watching your GPS update and change directions when you've made a wrong turn. Regulation of your cells, most oftentimes, is a benefit as it helps our bodies behave properly and aid us in adapting to our environment.

The Scientific Shift in Culpability

The idea of the *blame game* is something that we've seen from the beginning of time. We even spoke of it earlier in the book in regard to Adam and Eve. Science, and its advances in the study of the human body and human nature, have all too advanced the *blame game* status and have relegated personal culpability to nothing more than a load of nonsense. Studies from the 1980s and 1990s have ushered in a mentality of "our genes and/or our bodies made us do it." In 1987, Matti Virkkunen conducted studies on hypoglycemia whereby he noted that low blood sugar could be linked with truancy, low verbal IQ, tattooing, and stealing from home during childhood.[11] A few years later in 1998, Marcus Felson undertook similar research, where he opined that lowering daily sucrose intake in juvenile offenders made them less likely to have antisocial or aggressive behavior.[12] The studies in hypoglycemia research suggested that it wasn't the offender's fault, but their blood sugar made them do it, that the sexual assaults and motiveless murder could be chalked up to something biological . . . low blood sugar. I can hardly contain my urge to roll my eyes at that statement, and

---

11. Virkkunen, "Metabolic Dysfunctions Amongst Habitually Violent Offenders."

12. Felson, *Crime and Everyday Life*.

I would assume anyone else could hardly resist the urge either. It would be like saying that my husband's diabetes, when his sugar level drops drastically, can be the *root cause* of him committing a senseless crime. Doesn't that sound ridiculous? Do you believe that is a viable statement to make?

Other scientific studies and clinical trials advocated for the *blame game* as well, of course without the outright expression of their intent to do so. In 1987, Olweus[13] purportedly demonstrated that the physiological stressors of school life for juveniles only served to exacerbate aggressive behavior when it increased testosterone levels in young men.[14] Verbal and physical aggression, then, in young males was simply the result of stress and testosterone, not of their own lapse in moral character. In my mind, school would seemingly be the *lessor* stressor; I would dare say that video games result in verbal and physical aggression . . . at least my son's tireless efforts to annoy the entire family with his yelling while he plays *Call of Duty* with friends online is the culprit. But that's beside the point.

So, what does this have to do with crime and religion? It actually has a lot to do with it. Criminological theories (biosocial criminology) have been adapted to modern scientific advances, which serve to advance the idea that criminal culpability is involuntary . . . because our cells made us do it. It sounds quite ridiculous when you mention it out loud, but this theory prevails in many criminological circles. It is yet another feeble attempt to assign culpability elsewhere, other than the self. The bold statement that genetic disposition does not lead to criminal tendencies ushers in a pertinent question: *If the scientific endeavors of biosocial criminology become popular in society, and it has been established that there is evidence that genetics cause someone to commit a crime, what rights can be taken away from an individual who just so happens to possess a particular gene through no fault of their own?* From an ethical standpoint, this would strip away basic rights from the individual based on their genetic makeup. There are also other ethical issues with testing individuals and categorizing them by genetic makeup

13. Olweus, "Testosterone and Adrenaline."
14. Burke, *Contemporary Criminological Theory*, 47.

(think about sterilization, etc.), so let us not forget what history has taught us. One only has to look back to the 1930s to understand how sterilization made a major negative societal impact. Short of eugenics or genetic engineering, if criminal behavior has been determinatively biological or genetic, perhaps the best that society can hope for is to curb behavior by imprisonment until those offenders are no longer a threat to society, which (in reality) would be far more exhausting of an endeavor than one can imagine.

Remember just a few short pages ago when we talked about the biological and genetic nature of criminal behavior? Here are some situations to think through if we remove the idea of personal culpability in light of scientific studies.

First, let's take a look at *genetic predispositions for criminal behavior*. Suppose an individual is arrested for a crime that we would consider a capital crime (i.e., murder) and they argue that their genes made them do it. What are the questions that should be asked if someone has a gene, or is a carrier for a gene, that predisposes them to criminological behavior? If studies could prove to a reasonable scientific certainty that people were predisposed to criminal behavior, as a society, at what point do we start testing for this genetic predisposition? And would the testing for this disposition pose any ethical dilemmas? We must also consider, At what point do we advocate for the incarceration of a person for a crime they have not yet committed? And potentially may never commit? Would you want someone incarcerated, who is predisposed to a particular criminal behavior (yet may never commit that crime), who has the potential to molest, rape, or murder someone in your own family? Would you think this is ethical and advocate for their incarceration? What if *you* possessed this gene and were genetically predisposed to these more serious criminal acts? Should *you* be incarcerated? Also, at what point do we restrict civil liberties from people who have a genetic predisposition to crime?

Let's also consider the theory that *biological abnormalities are the cause of involuntary criminal behavior*. In the early 1800s, a German physician by the name of Franz Joseph Gall undertook anatomical studies of the brain in the search for biological causal links in the commission of crime. His theory of phrenology (the study of the shape of human skulls is a determining factor in a person's character and mental faculties), while inherently faulty, argued that mental faculties corresponded to different locations of the brain, which functioned independently of one another. In other words, some areas of the brain may function on a consistent basis, while others may not be used as much, therefore resulting in atrophy (breaking down) and constituting an abnormality in function. Criminal behavior, then, could be due to "the defective organization in those parts of the body, which are occupied by the oral faculties of the mind."[15] However, as mentioned before, Gall's work was inherently flawed. Technology was not as advanced as it is today, and Gall was unable to study the brain in depth. His theory of phrenology was based on physical attributes (bumps and hollows) of the human skull, not an in-depth look as we are able to have today.[16] The bumps and hollows, Gall said, were accurate indicators of the brain's functions. His studies, accepted in certain circles of medicine, thus characterized crime as a mental illness and treated criminal behavior as a sickness due to those abnormalities in bumps and hollows in the patients he studied. Therefore, the physical abnormalities were the contributing factors to criminological behavior, making that behavior involuntary. Normore and Fitch accurately noted the following, so it is worth quoting in its totality:

> More importantly, the idea that criminal behavior was the result of biological abnormalities meant that criminals were not responsible for their acts of deviance, a belief that later became the basis for the insanity defense found in modern court proceedings. This also inferred that crime, like other inheritable conditions, could be passed from generation to generation—and, therefore, only preventable through reproductive controls, which prevent such behavior, from being transmitted to future generations.[17]

15. Rush, *Medical Inquiries and Observations*, 360.
16. Sabbatini, "Phrenology"; see also Rush, *Medical Inquiries and Observations*, 360–65.
17. Normore and Fitch, *Leadership in Education*, 168.

This ideology poses the questions: Are bumps and hollows good indicators of mental faculty abnormalities? Do the deviations in bumps and hollows, from one individual to another, advocate for an involuntary mental illness that results in criminological behavior? If so, should we base the commission of crime on factors that differ drastically from one individual to another? Characteristics that differ drastically from one individual to another can also be extrapolated to factors such as skin color, eye color, and other physical deformities. Consider the question on this extrapolation: If someone suffers from achondroplasia (dwarfism), do they possess an involuntary nature to commit a crime over someone who does not have achondroplasia? If so, should all people with dwarfism be incarcerated even if they have not (yet) committed a crime? Is this ethical? Are there any moral dilemmas present in this mode of justice? This ideology of involuntary criminological behavior can be a slippery slope that leads to a whole slew of issues, including advancing the idea of segregation, a movement that we worked so hard to surpass.

CHRISTIAN ETHICS AND MODERN CRIME

There also exists a segue from science into Christian ethics as both are part and parcel of one another. In the realm of ethics, Christians hold to three major views: (1) reconstructionism, which insists on the death sentence for all serious crimes; (2) rehabilitationism, which does not allow for the death sentence at all; and (3) retributionism, which recommends death for some capital crimes.

Ethics and morality play a major role when it comes to the commission of crimes, and the Christian who holds to any of the above views is morally obligated to keep eternity in mind. There is certainly an element of eternal significance when considering the death penalty, or any penalty for a serious offense—one of the foundational tenets of Christian theology says that those who are not saved will go to hell. While Christians should consider eternity, justice should also be considered.

Retribution has many positive contributions and would be the most likely consideration for Christians in pursuit of upholding morality and ethical biblical standards. Each of the following are ideal positive contributions on the view itself: *Retribution is based on a high view of humanity.* This position presupposes a high view of human freedom and dignity. It is based on the assumption that adults are rational and moral beings who know right from wrong. *Retribution treats criminals with respect.* This is the "You get what you give principle." People who knowingly do wrong deserve to be punished, not to be treated like an object to be manipulated.

Retribution operates on a correct view of justice. The biblical worldview of justice is penal, not remedial. The primary purpose of justice is moral, not therapeutic. *Retribution does, in fact, deter crime.* Punishment deters crime (Deut 17:13) if the criminals see that their actions have consequences. Dead offenders cannot repeat their crimes. This is not to mean that all offenders are worthy of death or the death penalty. This is a simple statement that the physically dead cannot repeat their crimes, and the spiritually dead to modern ideals will *choose* not to commit crimes since God will hold their final judgment. And finally, going along with the previous statement, *retribution protects innocent lives.* Repeat crimes are not committed, and it puts the fear of God into would-be murderers.

There is a caveat, however, when it comes to retributionism—it ascribes the *degree of culpability* through which comes the extent of just punishment. In other words, "Retributivists look back at the criminal act and base their determination of appropriate sanctions on the nature of the *mens rea*, i.e., guilty mind, involved in the offence. When determining punishment, the retributive approach asks what kind of punishment the offender deserves, based on the extent of the person's responsibility for his or her actions."[18] If we solely base the punishment on the personal culpability of the offender, or the level of culpability in which they take responsibility, we must be careful to consider that these offenders will likely lie in order to obtain a lesser sentence. Some of the offenses

---

18. Gold and Applebaum, "Inclination to Evil," 163.

themselves beg the question on whether or not they are worthy of criminalization. This is seen as a "'sticky norm,' where there exists a gap between what the law regards as morally wrongful and what a significant segment of society views as such."[19] In other words, we must be careful (legislatively and morally) in meting out justice where the conduct is viewed as wrong, but maybe is not wrong *enough* to justify criminal penalties. Thus, the need for retributionist ideology.

Retributionist ideology, in and of itself, covers deterrence and protection of society for appropriately meting out justice to those who have decided they will abandon all morals and ethics in regard to human life. The views that appeal to rehabilitation of criminals (i.e., "redemptive criminology") ignore the fact that love and capital punishment are not contrary. If one takes the biblical worldview seriously, one will come to understand that love and punishment are the very principles behind capital punishment that made the cross necessary. The principle of "life for life" is the driving force behind substitutionary atonement. It takes life to atone for life (Lev 17:11), and that notion is what makes capital punishment necessary for capital crimes. In fact, if capital punishment hadn't been enacted in the first century, then Jesus would not have died for our sins. Capital punishment and other serious forms of sentence, from a biblical perspective, thus elevate the value of life rather than degrading it. It is incumbent upon the Christian and any individual who believes in a moral code to uphold the value of life by inciting the proper form of punishment and admonishing personal culpability.

CASE STUDIES IN MODERN CRIME

The "subject of religion should be a more prominent feature of criminological theory and research for the straightforward reason that many of the core concerns of criminology—deviance, morality, punishment, rehabilitation—are also, in one way or another,

---

19. Green, *Lying, Cheating, and Stealing*, 24.

central to religion."[20] However, much of the study on modern crime (post-1900s) is in criminal theory and understanding how and where crime "hotspots" happen. In other words, American criminology has had a tendency to focus on units of analysis that included communities, ethnicities, and microgeographic crime hotspots.[21] This emphasis paved the way for examining why crime occurred in certain places and in certain communities, all the while shifting the focus away from *why* specific people commit crime. The shift away from the root of the problem has been seen in multiple scholarly resources, such as books like *Critical Criminology Today: Counter Hegemonic Essays* by Vincenzo Ruggiero, *Gendering Criminology* by Shelly Clevenger and Jordana N. Navarro, and even *Women's Drug Use in Everyday Life* by Emma Eleonorasdotter. Many works like these focus on the outlying factors that many criminals use as a handicap, or a ledge, on which to rest their culpability instead of their own selfishness and greed. American culture has perpetuated a scapegoat mentality also when it comes to crime and gender—giving into the idea that if genders can be fluid, so can the reasons for crime. This may seem like a gross extrapolation; however, it is very relevant as gender lenses on criminology are becoming all too prevalent.[22]

It is my opinion that in this shift there is an inherent flaw, one that eradicates the need for personal culpability. The shift from personal culpability, i.e., selfishness, that drives crime is now blamed on poverty, ethnicity, social status, and the like. These are the very issues that remain at the forefront of modern political debates and run the gamut resulting in riots and hatred of other people groups. The root of the problem is evil (1 Tim 6:9–10) and

20. Durrant and Poppelwell, *Religion, Crime and Punishment*, 16.

21. Weisburd, "Law of Crime Concentration," 133. See also Laub, "Life Course of Criminology."

22. While this is not a *new* area of study or focus in criminology, gender has been at the forefront of many scientific and sociological studies in the modern day (post-2000). Publications in the form of journal articles and books all make reference to gender lenses, especially as it relates to criminological theory. A major source for reference is Britton, Jacobsen, and Howard, *Gender of Crime*.

selfishness (Jas 3:16). Even in Gen 3:12–13, Adam blamed Eve and then Eve blamed the serpent: "The man said, 'The woman whom You gave to be with me, she gave me the fruit of the Tree and I ate.' Then the LORD God said to the woman, 'What is this that you have done?' The woman said, 'The serpent deceived me, and I ate.'" The realization that greed and selfishness are at the core of criminal activity in no way demeans or dismisses those things like poverty, ethnic backgrounds, genders, and social statuses as they indeed play a role in the influence of crime. Our point is that those things are *not the root cause*.

The following case studies are *real cases*. Names and locations have been changed to protect the privacy of all the individuals involved. Each case study highlights people from a different background, gender, and economic status. And each case study attests to the fact that crime is not influenced by these factors; crime is perpetuated from the idea of "wanting," meaning selfishness. The questions at the end of each case study serve to help you think through the issues and correctly address the situation from a law enforcement perspective. My husband, and contributor to this book, has been in law enforcement for the past twenty-six years. He's held the positions of jailer, patrolman, investigator, death investigator, and even school resource officer. His expertise in the field far surpasses mine. The following are cases he has had experience with or someone he knows has had experience with. Read the case studies carefully and assess how *you* would deal with the situation. And, ultimately, ask yourself: "Does the background really matter?"

Case Study #1

A mid-day phone call to the investigations division at the local sheriff's office from a prominent public official raised some eyebrows that day. A fraud scheme had purportedly been in the works for the past year on the part of the public official's secretary. The kicker in the scheme was that the secretary was in her mid-sixties. Investigators found that she had been skimming money from her public official employer by way of retainer fees, totaling a dismal amount of seven thousand dollars. While she intended to only make "ends meet" by skimming a few hundred dollars here and there, and to pay the money back, the money eventually began to add up and the feeling of not being in debt got the better of her. So, she kept on her scheme with the "comforting" thought that no one would catch on to her greed. But someone did notice . . . her boss.

As minor as this crime may seem, it boils down to selfishness . . . and selfishness and greed of someone described by the community as a "godly church woman" at that. She had been serving as the secretary of a local Baptist church, whose eyebrows also must have been raised at the news of her confession and impending arrest.

Ultimately, she was charged with "theft by taking while under a fiduciary obligation," which basically means that, by being in a position of trust, she had an obligation by law to handle the money of that business in the best interests of her employer. Stealing money was certainly not in the best interests of the employer.

Her greed and selfishness in theft from her employer and the people who entrusted that business with their money resulted in a felony charge on her record. Her background served her well in getting the job initially: no criminal history, actively involved in church, and an all-around "great woman" if you'd stop and ask someone about her on the street. All this to say that she was motivated by greed, a subconscious glottal stop (if you will) on the morality scale. She needed money and she found a way to take it. Her background didn't make her do it, her lapse in moral code did. She chose to commit a crime, and she ultimately paid the price for it. A felony stamp on her permanent record, she can no longer own a firearm or do her duty as a citizen and vote. Greed transcends age, social status, and economic factors. It does not discriminate, but we must remember that the law doesn't discriminate either . . . it is applicable to each and every one of us, and it is our duty to choose to follow it.

What could she have done to make ends meet instead of stealing from her employer? Was greed a factor in this case? Or was there another motivation you can point to? Why would you say this is important to understand? Do you think that because she was a prominent and, in some ways, privileged citizen that she should not have been charged with a felony? Why or why not? Do you think "crime" and "sin" are interchangeable terms? Why or why not?

Case Study #2

During the months of May through July 2024, a national kidnapping case had made its way across the news in the United States. A young, twelve-year-old Hispanic girl from Hall County, Georgia, had gone missing.[23] We are talking about this case because it happened in my home state, and its many facets raise questions when it comes to crime, criminality, religion, morals, etc. Really, it just runs the gamut. No details have been changed in this study since it was nationally publicized.

Most of you might have heard the story. Twelve-year-old Maria Gomez-Perez, from Gainesville, Georgia, went missing from her home on May 29, 2024. Her family had feared that she had been abducted and pressed the community and authorities to keep searching for their daughter. Community members even rallied together to help amass a fifty thousand dollar reward for her safe return. As time ticked by, the family had come to terms with the fear that she might be dead, but they still held on to the hope that one day she would be returned to them safely.

Their prayers and community efforts had paid off, but the major player in the game was Maria herself. News outlets began reporting that the girl (who had been taken to Dover, Ohio) contacted her father via social media to let him know that she was all right, but to "stop looking for her" and that "she wasn't coming home." While this may seem odd to some, Maria had been communicating with multiple older males online through Facebook Messenger about how unhappy she was at home. This led to her

---

23. The following facts come from Fingert, "Maria Gomez-Perez Found Safe"; and Daughtry, "Reward for Missing 12-Year-Old."

"abductor" driving all the way from Ohio to Gainesville, Georgia, to pick her up.

Investigators from Hall County, Georgia, tracked the IP address of the computer she used to communicate with her father and found that it was registered to a particular area in Dover, Ohio. Investigators then traveled to Ohio and found Maria with a Guatemalan national, who was later arrested and held in the Tuscarawas County Jail on multiple felony charges.

At the time of writing this book, the Guatemalan national is still being held in the Tuscarawas County Jail. Once he is processed there and charged, his extradition back to Hall County, Georgia, will commence. Looking at the (very) brief synopsis of events in this case, what questions come into play? Was a crime committed? Can the child in the case be morally culpable for her actions, or is there an age requirement? If not, why? What risk do we run when we remove culpability even at a young age?

Case Study #3

Back in 2015, law enforcement officers responded to a report of a structure fire where an individual had been severely burned. The victim had been transported to the hospital for her injuries, which were third-degree burns all over her body. The maintenance man had called in the "boom" he heard coming from her mobile home, the *same* man who had come into her home earlier in the *same* day to replace a leaking gas line in her stove.

The woman's gas line in her mobile home was left uncapped, meaning that the natural gas (which is heavier than air) began to sink to the floor and, while the windows were closed, slowly built up in layers. Smelling gas while she was on the phone with her mother, her mother advised her to open the windows, thus allowing the gas to dissipate into the outside environment. After a few hours, the woman closed her windows again, allowing the gas to build up in layers, all unbeknownst to her. The stove's pilot light, which had been relit by the maintenance man earlier in the day, was the second factor needed in the chain of events that caused the explosion of her home. Once the natural gas reached the level of the stove's pilot light (an open flame), the explosion happened and severely burned the woman and subsequently melted all of her clothes to her body. She was transferred emergent to the Grady Burn Unit in Atlanta by Georgia Air Life. Upon further investigation by the sheriff's office and the fire investigator, a portable heater was also found sitting near the open natural gas line in her home, which likely contributed to the severity of her burns.

Here comes the kicker in the whole scenario. The maintenance man's work was on a case-by-case contract with the mobile home park he was employed by. In a last-ditch effort to make money, he decided he would de-fraud the trailer park owner and disassemble parts of individual mobile homes when people moved out, so he would, in turn, have to be called on to fix it, thus "earning" him his wage, when in fact he was really stealing in the grand scheme of things.

In the case of the "boom" that had been heard, the woman was living in a trailer that the maintenance man had cut the gas off to. The second kicker is that *this was the home that the maintenance man himself had just moved out of.* In his vacancy of the property, he in turn cut off the line to the heater on the wall in the home. In doing so, he did not cap the gas lines to prevent leakage should the gas lines ever get turned back on. Eventually, when the woman's stove wasn't working, the maintenance man did not fix the gas lines but instead lit the stove's pilot light and went about his day. Whether this was negligence, carelessness, or something else, questions should have been raised about his "quick fix."

The maintenance man not only exhibited a negligent attitude in regard to his job and the safety of the people he serves—greed and fraud were the major factors as to why this man did this—but in this instance, his actions cost someone their life. My husband was one of the investigators in this case. While he mentions that the man who was charged with involuntary manslaughter in the woman's untimely death didn't *mean* to kill anyone, his actions of greed and underhandedness took her life. Unfortunately, the maintenance man only served one year in prison. In your opinion, and based on the facts presented for the case study, did he own up to his actions? Did he view himself as personally culpable for her death? Was what he was doing morally or ethically wrong?

CASE STUDIES: FINAL THOUGHTS

Imagine you're reading a newspaper article on someone who committed a murder. Do you need to know the background of that person to understand what the crime was that they committed? That should be a resounding NO! The background facts always help the investigator *understand why* the person did what they did, but those facts don't really help anything in the long run; they only serve to influence the criminal in their decision to go against the moral code. The motivation, then, is of pure selfishness as seen in the case studies we presented above.

Regardless of someone's biblical convictions, or non-convictions, there exists a universal moral code of what is good and what is evil. The consciousness that embodies what personhood *is* reveals that moral code on the subconscious level. And while backgrounds, social situations, and even gender can influence decision-making, the very foundation of crime is greed and selfishness. Some have argued that crime and sin should not be used interchangeably, but playing semantics on the moral code poses some serious questions. Just because "many crimes are not sins, and many sins are not crimes"[24] does not mean that the two don't go hand-in-hand. The sinful heart leads to sinful acts, some of which just happen to be criminal.

Remember the comment made in a previous chapter about the culpability in penal trials? Restorative justice plays on the moral codes, one of the reasons criminal trials exist. They are not only to serve punishment and uphold the standards of the community, but they also serve to play on that personal culpability, or at least seek to (in some ways) instill that ideology of personal culpability in the offender. The criminal trial has been said to be

24. Griffith, *Fall of the Prison*, 186.

a "degradation ceremony."[25] These degradation ceremonies, in the spirit of retributive justice, transform the identity of the criminal into something deemed *lesser* in the social realm, "through the moral indignation of the group and resulting public denunciation of the offender."[26] In other words, the former self is done away with, and the new criminal emerges . . . essentially blooming into the person that they were all along.

As I opine about the transformative process in ritual criminological trials, the morality code would be enough for me to change my behavior. Yet, for a large percentage of offenders, it has no effect. The pull of sinful, immoral behaviors is too strong for their ever-struggling wills. When one engages in immoral conduct, it is evident that the individual often finds the support necessary to justify their actions, which in turn justifies the underlying questioning conscience. "In those instances when further justification is required, the human mind is capable of generating an extraordinary set of rationalizations, many of which excuse and, in some cases, even celebrate misconduct."[27]

The idea of personal culpability in light of modern-day issues almost seems insignificant; if anything, some criminals (especially those involved in gang culture) vie for public "humiliation" as it serves to only highlight their misdeeds and elevate their status within their groups. That stigma of shame, or humiliation, is often deeply internalized by the offender and the incarceration *ritual* (which the offender rotates in and out of) almost becomes part of their *identity*. Frank Tannenbaum noted, "He [the offender] becomes conscious of himself as a different human being than he was before his arrest; he becomes the thing he is described as being."[28] Thus, he decides to follow the immoral path and live up to the "offender" name and mentality. In a sense, he owns up to the immoral laws . . . he *owns* the immoral laws. His identity is then bound up in immorality, yet he is praised for his immoral practices by his

25. Garfinkel, "Conditions of Successful Degradation Ceremonies," 421.
26. Pointer, *Restorative Justice Ritual*, 41.
27. Normore and Fitch, *Leadership in Education*, 12.
28. Tannenbaum, *Crime and the Community*, 20.

peers. If one can own up to immoral practices, being personally culpable for the crimes they choose to commit, why is it that personal culpability is not owned up to in legal proceedings? What is the difference between the street and the courtroom? The prison yard and the interrogation room?

Chapter Five

The Officer

His Duty and Ethics

The integrity of the upright will guide them, but the perversity of the unfaithful will destroy them.

—PROVERBS 11:3

UPHOLDING THE OFFICER'S OATH

WHEN ONE ACCEPTS THE call to serve his or her community through the field of law enforcement, they take an oath to protect and defend their respective communities. The *generic* law enforcement oath of honor reads: "On my honor, I will never betray my *integrity*, my character, or the public trust. I will always have the courage to hold myself and others *accountable for our actions*. I will always maintain the highest *ethical standards* and uphold the *values* of my community, and the agency I serve."[1]

In the state of Georgia, law enforcement officers are sworn in with the following oath of office: "I will faithfully execute all writs,

---

1. International Association of Chiefs of Police, "Oath of Honor" (emphasis mine).

warrants, precepts, and processes directed to me as a Deputy Sheriff of the County, or which are directed to all Sheriffs of this State, or to any other Sheriff specially, which I can lawfully execute, and true returns make, and in all things well and truly, without malice or partiality, perform the duties of the Office of Deputy Sheriff of [insert county], during my continuance therein, and take only my lawful fees."[2]

The oath of office implies a discretionary authority on the part of the officer, and that discretionary authority, in turn, implies the officer act in an unbiased, moral, and ethical manner when it comes to their interactions with offenders. The law itself, unfortunately, cannot enforce all aspects of morality that concern preventing harm to others. In fact, many immoral acts are unregulated by the law. Yet, while the law may be seen as a crude instrument in some cases, it is incumbent upon the law enforcement professional to extend "a matter of prudential judgment or some kind of balancing of morally relevant factors"[3] in their daily dealings with offenders in order to promote ethics, morality, and personal culpability. Ethics and duty are then born out of a moral code, but the question remains, Are ethics and duty morally compatible?

ETHICS AND DUTY—MORAL COMPATIBILITY?

Ethical behavior forms the foundation for any professional organization. Law enforcement is no different; it operates out of a broad ethical spectrum that seeks to cover all divisions equally. However, a broad ethical spectrum falls short in the real-world scenarios of policing. One cannot address all divisions the same—patrol will have different needs and priorities than the investigations division, just as the jail division will have different needs and priorities than the narcotics division. Thus, the needs and priorities of each division call for a different ethical and moral code (in theory) in order to carry out specific duties. It has even been acknowledged, from

---

2. A special thank you to the sheriff of my county for providing this statement from his files. His name will not be shared due to confidentiality matters.

3. Greenawalt, "Legal Enforcement of Morality," 711.

antiquity, that "the perception of honorable behavior and actions is not uniform across all cultures; instead they are relative based on the culture surrounding the society in judgment."[4] This statement exemplifies the broad ethical spectrum that encompasses police work. For example, "a code of conduct that addresses all divisions through a single code may state that it is unacceptable for an officer to lie. Yet, an officer working in an undercover narcotics capacity is expected to immerse himself into the criminal element to be able to buy drugs. If someone trying to sell an undercover officer drugs, questions if the buyer is a police officer, he will not be successful if he answers that question truthfully."[5] From this example, one might find the basis to argue that immoral behaviors (i.e., behaviors that are not socially acceptable in mainstream society) are justified if they are performed within the capacity of police work.

Police work calls for questionable morals, at times, and the officers are faced with making these hard decisions on a daily basis, some even on a second-by-second basis; there is no telling how an event might transpire. The job is not only physically and mentally exhausting but emotionally exhausting as well. As all individuals are endowed with a conscience that guides us in the "right and wrong" of decision making, it is sometimes hard for the law enforcement officer to disrupt the moral code in favor of "doing the right thing" and getting criminals off the streets. All too often, however, the longer someone serves in the law enforcement profession, they may have the tendency to succumb to immoral behaviors. The practices of lying, deception, threats of force, and the depravation of personal liberty are all things that are seen as morally and ethically acceptable while performing the duty of a law enforcement officer. However, "the use of these methods by police officers in circumstances, which are morally justified, can begin to have a corrupting influence upon the individuals who make use of them."[6] This morally inept behavior and *choice* can be seen as an occupational hazard and should be trained on; some

    4. Isaac, "For Such a Time as This," 60.
    5. Dutelle and Taylor, *Ethics for the Public Service Professional*, 58.
    6. Dutelle and Taylor, *Ethics for the Public Service Professional*, 58.

have offered the suggestion to train police officers on moral vulnerability as well, since morality and ethics form the very basis of their work. Emphasis should be placed on corporate morality and responsibility as an accountability basis for law enforcement officers as it "reinforces the need for and acceptance of proper moral decision making."[7]

Corporate morality in law enforcement should not hinge on force, authority, or coercion. Corporate morality should function like corporate worship—cultivating the heart's inclinations toward God and truthfulness. "Such inclinations are shaped most significantly through habitual behavior in community," which serves "to incarnate biblical values and transmit them to the worshiper/disciple. When the liturgies of corporate worship are reenactments of what God has done in the gospel, these liturgies help to make disciples, for by reenacting what they are in Christ, Christian worshipers become what they are."[8] In other words, liturgies should be akin to the moral accountabilities in the law enforcement profession whereby officers *choose* to uphold peace, truth, and righteousness through their actions and decisions . . . and not let the moral lapses that are deemed acceptable on the job influence their life outside of the profession.

So, are ethics and duty morally compatible? I would say that they are. The hard truth is that law enforcement personnel, in the long run, must act like the criminal to deter or detain the criminal. Law enforcement officers (and really anyone who works in public safety) are constantly exposed to the worst of what society has to offer. This does not excuse unethical or immoral behavior off the clock, but it does contribute to it. Not only does the officer have to wrestle with their own demons when it comes to truth, ethics, morality, and everything in-between, but they have to wrestle with the criminals who chose *willingly* to commit acts contradictory to common sense and conscience.

---

7. Dutelle and Taylor, *Ethics for the Public Service Professional*, 75.
8. Aniol, "Practice Makes Perfect," 93.

OATH, PUNISHMENT, AND REPENTANCE

To no man will we refuse justice.

—Magna Carta

"Legal systems characteristically, even if not essentially, rely on the threat of punishment. In the world in which we live, legal efforts to regulate conduct and to guide it in morally desirable directions must impose criminal punishments to be effective."[9] In classical and neoclassical criminology, we saw that Bentham and Beccaria advanced the idea that punishments—both logistical and conceptual—should be proportional to the crime. Beccaria's "treatises" on punishment ultimately ensured that punishment should not be an act of violence.[10]

There is a tendency, in modern law enforcement, to enact violence for what one would consider violent crimes. And while certain crimes invoke a state of passion among law enforcement officers, a feeling of rage and incredulity at the same time, we must consider Nietzsche's position for the offenders, "(excessive) pain is not simply productive but innate to humanity, and the joy occasioned in its application."[11] Eradicating problems of injustice, from a law enforcement officer's viewpoint, would stem from adopting some of classical and neoclassical thought. Enacting Nietzsche's ideology that crime is bound up in moral code[12] ought to be critically assessed from a biblical or even quasi-biblical standpoint. Steven Wall surmises:

> Since legal systems do and ought to enforce morality, the interesting question is not whether the law should enforce morality. The interesting questions concern what parts of morality the law ought to enforce, the considerations that justify its enforcement, how the law ought to enforce morality, the relationship between the legal and social

---

9. Wall, *Enforcing Morality*, 1.
10. Beccaria, *Essay on Crimes*, 81.
11. Ranasinghe, "Friedrich Nietzsche, *On the Genealogy of Morals*," 89.
12. Nietzsche, *On the Genealogy of Morals*.

enforcement of morality and whether there are moral limits that constrain the enforcement of morality—and, if so, the nature and justifications for these limits.[13]

"In the criminal justice sphere, with the threat of punishment, proceeding with the knowledge that no one is to blame is morally repugnant even though the authorities can face horrendous pressure to act when a major incident occurs."[14] In all contexts, biblical and non-biblical, "blame is an evaluative response but it is not simply an objective evaluation, it is connected to desire, emotion, expectation and disposition . . . the blamer is doing more than simply making an objective entry on some form of moral ledger. Blame is linked to resentment, but it is a distinctive emotional response."[15] Adam and Eve were to blame for their own actions, but they placed blame elsewhere as they likely *resented* their actions. Deuteronomy 25:16 undoubtedly bolsters this idea in that it espouses "only for their own crimes may persons be put to death." Scripture advocates for this personal culpability in its calls for a return to righteousness. Ezekiel 18:30–32 states that the LORD takes no pleasure in the death of his people and calls each and every individual to take responsibility for their actions before him and turn from their evil ways. Repentance, then, is a responsibility before God—an essential—to prevent the iniquity (or crime) from being one's ruin.

CHANGING DYNAMICS

Early criminal laws, as noted throughout the book, were marked by (and rooted in) a decidedly religious character.[16] "Today's law, however, appears to have lost this ancient character. Making a causal connection between our criminal law and religious commands is a habit we are widely regarded as having outgrown. Time

---

13. Wall, *Enforcing Morality*, 1.
14. Dingwall and Hillier, *Blamestorming*, 154.
15. Dingwall and Hillier, *Blamestorming*, 155.
16. Maine, *Ancient Law*, 1–19.

and opinion move on. Religion now belongs within the private side of modern lives, not the public world of courts and crime."[17] Changing the dynamics of the criminal justice system comes with the inception of "redemptive criminology," as mentioned back in chapter 1.

> Criminal justice practice as a project of modernity has relied increasingly on the use of "hard," medico-reductionist, "psy" disciplines (psychology and psychiatry) because they seem to offer scientific objectivity and clarity of meaning, which can then underpin and justify treatment programmes and managerial accountability. The superiority of these approaches is asserted over the "soft," socially complex, "re" disciplines (rehabilitation, restoration and redemption), which appear too uncertain and contradictory.[18]

In other words, criminology and understanding criminals in light of individual nature centers largely on the natural and foundational aspects of theology, philosophy, and ethics, in that the "resources for ethical and normative practice as the dynamics of change come from the bottom up."[19] Each of these reveals the freedom of choice, or free will that theologian Dietrich Bonhoeffer spoke of, in that we are not seeking freedom from others, but *for others* . . . just as God does for us.[20] Thus, the beginning of redemption lies not in the statutes and laws of the state, but within the moral code that God has instilled since creation.

There have been arguments that one cannot legislate the moral code, however. The Prohibition Era (Eighteenth Amendment of the United States Constitution) is commonly used as such an example that we should not even try to legislate morality. Newman Enyioko notes:

> Every law is a legislation of someone's morality. Murder and theft are moral issues. Enacting laws against these

17. Hill, "Introduction," 1.
18. Pycroft and Bartollas, *Redemptive Criminology*, 1.
19. Pycroft and Bartollas, *Redemptive Criminology*, 97.
20. McBride and Fabisiak, "Bonhoeffer's Critique of Morality," 89–110.

actions is a legislation of morality. The important question is, "whose morality should we legislate?" There are really only two answers: either God's morality (which He reveals in His Word, the Bible) or man's. While all law legislates morality, it is very important to understand that man cannot legislate goodness. Laws cannot change the heart of man; they cannot elevate men above the level of their faith and morality.[21]

Crime flourishes because "if civil government does not fulfill its duty to restrain criminals in accordance with Biblical guidelines, then crime will flourish. Ecclesiastes 8:11 says, 'Because the sentence against an evil deed is not executed quickly, therefore the hearts of the sons of men among them are given fully to do evil.' Swift execution of God's justice is necessary to keep a culture of crime from growing in a nation."[22] In essence, it only takes a small step to enact change—for instance, something so small and so seemingly insignificant as a butterfly flapping its wings can affect change on the other side of the world (see chaos theory and/or the butterfly effect). This principle, then, can be applied in the legislation of morality in law enforcement as a catalyst for change to enact fairness and equality when it comes to ethics and duty. Laws are thus a reflection of society's general consensus of morality.

ADVOCATING FOR A FAIR TRIAL

Amendment 14, section 1 of the United States Constitution notes that "no State shall . . . deny to any person within its jurisdiction the equal protection of the laws," which stands in line with the biblical text of Deut 1:16–17: "I charged your judges at that time: 'Give the members of your community a fair hearing, and judge rightly between one person and another, whether citizen or resident alien. You must not be partial in judging: hear out small and the great alike; you shall not be intimidated by anyone, for the judgment is God's.'" Both of these statements carry much weight.

21. Enyioko, "Security Constitution."
22. Enyioko, "Security Constitution."

It is incumbent on the officer's part, no matter what they personally feel in their interactions with criminal offenders, to advocate for a fair trial. Stuart P. Green advises that fairness and morality are complementary facets of the legal system whereby

> determining whether, and to what extent, the commission of a given crime entails moral fault is crucial to determining whether, and how much, punishment should be imposed. Moreover, without an adequate grounding in widely held moral values, the criminal law loses its legitimacy. If the criminal sanction is overused, or misused, its potency is dilute, its sting is lost, and it is ultimately rendered ineffective. Assessing the moral content of criminal law is thus also an essential step in assessing its likely effectiveness.[23]

The importance of impartial judgment stands at the forefront of Western jurisprudence and also at the forefront of biblical jurisprudence. The Bible gives a stern warning to "keep far from false charges" (Exod 23:7); this implication "seems to be that if there was any serious question as to the truth of adverse evidence in a capital case, the accused should be spared execution; moreover that YHWH himself would attend to the just fate of the real offender, whether the accused or some other person."[24] This idea of fair trial, no matter if it is an earthly or heavenly trial, also can be seen in the example of Sodom and Gomorrah in a previous chapter; it expressly challenges the propriety of punishing the innocent along with the guilty, hinging on the precepts of a moral code.[25]

Officers are the "upholders" of the Holiness Code and the Covenant Code. Their oaths are dependent on meting out justice and doing what is *right*. The Holiness Code notes that one shall not *be partial . . . but in righteousness shall you judge your neighbor* (Lev 19:15), while the Covenant Code says that *you shall not pervert justice* and *take no bribes* (Exod 23:3, 6–8). The officer's oath, then, requires adherence to biblical morality mandates. Its importance

---

23. Green, *Lying, Cheating, and Stealing*, 22.
24. Hiers, *Justice and Compassion in Biblical Law*, 74.
25. Hiers, *Justice and Compassion in Biblical Law*, 74.

THE OFFICER

hinges on the words of Prov 18:5: "It is not right to be partial to the guilty, or to subvert the innocent in judgment." Even the Magna Carta, the document that placed governmental limits on royal authority, noted that *to no man will we refuse justice.*

BOTTOM LINES AND HARD TRUTHS

"Cultures that strongly emphasize 'law and order,' along with being highly stigmatizing, tend to nurture criminal subcultures: they create a market for an oppositional identity."[26] While the demands on local law enforcement agencies are always at an all-time-high, there are routes to rehabilitation and ways to meet the needs of citizens in a meaningful way, all the while serving to deter criminological behavior. Behavior, in and of itself, is partially a function of unmet needs. "The decision to commit a crime is often evidence of a need the person is attempting to fulfill, though the way of doing it is harmful to others. Therefore, a process that allows for the exploration of the needs behind behavior can lead to important societal change."[27] Implementing community programs that deter violence and help to create fewer victims (like women's self-defense classes, community firearms courses, etc.) should be at the forefront of community outreach efforts.

In an effort to promote a safe community, the "Broken Windows" theory should be taken more seriously. Advocated by Wilson and Kelling in 1982, the "Broken Windows" theory really served as a metaphor for communities in decline . . . or the *reason* for community decline. Just as broken windows, left untended for some time, are a sign that no one cares and eventually invites more broken windows, so disorderly behavior left untended is a sign that nobody cares and creates a culture of criminological behavior.[28] All of this leads to urban decay and an influx in crime. If law enforcement could control and/or prevent crime with policy,

---

26. Pointer, *Restorative Justice Ritual*, 48.
27. Pointer, *Restorative Justice Ritual*, 50.
28. Sousa and Kelling, "Of 'Broken Windows,'" 121–22.

that would be the ideal. Policymakers would love to live in a world where "they were 95 percent certain that implementing particular policies or practices would have the desired outcome.... Policymakers live in a world in which they have to make decisions—many of them, life and death—in which they are confronted with mixes of problems and programs that do not lend themselves to clean experiments, bad data, and often conflicting and/or uncertain research findings."[29] Thus, this leaves law enforcement officers with only the immediate life and death decision making, which is based on their knowledge, training, and experience in the field. To combat criminal behavior on the streets and to make policy while sitting in a safe office atmosphere are two completely different things. While policies help, it comes down to the officers on the front lines who deal with the criminal one-on-one. Policy allows the officer to enact the laws and hold the criminals personally culpable for their crimes, but the policies are not always foolproof, and they are not always what's best morally.

ADVOCATING FREE WILL

All people take an ethical stance on what is right and what is wrong. The existence and nature of free will is a matter of practical importance for how we will employ an ethical perspective in our individual and social dealings with others. The issue of free will is seen through two lenses—compatibilist and libertarian freedom. Compatibilist freedom asserts, "If determinism [for every event that happens, there are conditions such that, given them, nothing else could have happened] is true, then every human action is causally necessitated by events that obtained prior to the action, including events that existed before the person acting was born."[30] This means that actions humans do are just mere happenings—they are parts of causal chains of events that lead up to them in a deterministic fashion. Freedom is compatible with determinism.

29. Sousa and Kelling, "Of 'Broken Windows,'" 138.
30. Moreland, "Science, Miracles, Agency Theory," 137.

Classical compatibilism argues for a bodily freedom, whereas hierarchical compatibilism places an emphasis on freedom of the will. It seems that this position is saying, on very basic levels, that free will and divine sovereignty work together (but obviously more is going on, too). Libertarian freedom asserts that the freedom necessary for responsible action is not compatible with determinism. Real freedom requires a type of control over one's actions—and, more importantly, over one's will—such that given a choice to do A or B, nothing determines that either choice is made. This means that the person exercises his own free will and "causal powers" to do one thing over the other. The person who is doing the action is the sole originator of his actions; this theory is then both a position on free will and a theory about the nature of agents (the human) and agency.[31]

In a world where policing is a high-risk occupation for misconduct (both for the offender and the officer), the exercise of free will in demanding circumstances rests solely on the moral code of the individual. Some scientists have argued that free will is simply an illusion, whereby no individual has control over their behaviors as they are pre-determined (or pre-programmed) and that "free will is only something we assume when we do not know the causes of behaviours."[32] Yet, both the officer and the offender's behaviors are judged according to moral and ethical codes, assuming that free will is being exercised in the choices they make.

While it may seem like ethical dilemmas exist in the law enforcement profession, and I might argue that sometimes they do, regarding the decisions to be made "on the fly," there do not exist ethical dilemmas in the criminal world, as the choices they make are completely self-satisfying and disregard all moral and ethical codes in spite of reason. The element of self-satisfaction or self-gratification (a.k.a. "the sin nature") functions as the override button of life. Therefore, the law enforcement officer must make sound judgments based on an underlying moral code that

31. Kane, *Significance of Free Will*, 4.
32. Prenzler, *Ethics and Accountability in Criminal Justice*, 3; Pollock, *Ethical Dilemmas and Decisions*, 10–23.

has been written on the hearts of men (Rom 2:15–16), and the offender has to comes to terms with the choices he makes and hold himself personally responsible no matter what the outcome of his actions may be (Gal 5:13; Rom 13:2).

Chapter Six

Conclusion

Do not fail to do good even if it's small;
do not engage in evil even if it's small.

—Zhu Ge Liang from "Chu Shi Biao"

The quote above, from the imperial chancellor of the state of Shu during the Three Kingdoms period in China, serves as a fervent reminder for law enforcement officials today. We live in a secular world that is full of personality, opinions, political stances, and much more. It is as colorful and complicated as one can possibly imagine. Within this socially complex sphere exist multiple religions and religious beliefs. Religion pervades every area of humanity, and some hold more tightly and more fervently to it than others.

Regardless of personal opinions or biases, there exist Judeo-Christian underpinnings of creation and creative aspects when it comes to the design and individuality of what it means to be human. The ancient philosophers sought to understand personhood, and modern scholars have continued to scientifically quantify its characteristics. Morality was, and has continued to be, the one foundational block in understanding who we are and why we exist. As mentioned throughout the pages of this short work, individuals have been endowed with a moral consciousness that drives everyday decision-making. Societal factors such as age, gender, culture, economic status, and the like have played a part in the decisions individuals make and their decisions, especially in relation to criminological activity. The driving force behind that criminological activity is the desire to pursue a momentary pleasure, or in some cases, a momentary pain. Understanding that it is our duty to take personal responsibility for our actions could potentially usher in a new era for law enforcement and rehabilitation.

THE PRACTICAL BASIS

Sir Robert Peel, the father of modern-day policing, reformed the police and founded the Metropolitan Police service in London. In his "Nine Principles of Policing," he noted that the authority of the police comes from society's acceptance and willingness to let officers enforce it. As the harbingers of moral code, law enforcement retains the right to exercise a moral code of conduct on every citizen. No personal rights are being infringed upon either (to some chagrin of those who choose to act immorally). The police can do their job, because the public in general allows them to do so. Officers regularly construct their "work in terms of a morality that is so pronounced that it must arise from unique aspects of their role in society."[1] Steve Herbert notes:

> Three components of the police function create potent dilemmas that their morality helps ameliorate: the contradiction between the police's ostensible aim to prevent crime and their inability to do so; the imperative that they run roughshod over the ambiguity inherent in most situations they handle; and the fact that they invariably act against at least one citizen's interest, often with recourse to a coercive force that can maim or kill. Reliance on

1. Herbert, "Morality in Law Enforcement," 799.

moralistic understandings for the police's mission provides a salve for these difficulties; however, it can also work to harm police-community relations. Paradoxically, the police's reliance on morality can encourage or condone overly aggressive actions that are, in fact, contradictory to the virtuous self-definition officers often construct.[2]

As a common rule, regardless of the religious implications or beliefs of the individual, legal systems enforce morality. It is not a disputed fact "that the development of law, at all times and places, has in fact been profoundly influenced both by the conventional morality and ideals of particular social groups, and also by forms of enlightened moral criticism urged by individuals, whose moral horizon has transcended the morality currently accepted."[3]

Changing Behavior

It can be argued that human error is normal, expected behavior. But the type of human error serves as a characterization of the human in question. As such, there is an increasing demand and call to action for individuals who commit crimes to be held accountable; yet even in the criminal justice process, there exists the realization that attributing blame is not a value-neutral process. It seems almost contradictory to say that the criminal justice system can place blame on an individual, but the reality of it is that the system exists for a reason, to draw out the moral culpability of the offenders in question. If society, then, wanted a change in the system of bringing to light the moral responsibility of the criminals it processes on the daily, then it would be incumbent upon them to find a strategy and "make it happen."

From antiquity to the modern world, laws have changed because a group of people were not happy with the moral, ethical, or judicial tenets passed in their legislation. When the United States of America was founded in 1776, many of the laws had their roots in Christianity, as that was the prevalent religion brought

2. Herbert, "Morality in Law Enforcement," 799.
3. Hart, *Concept of Law*, 185.

over from England and subsequently established as the basis of American law. In other words, basic laws were derived from the Ten Commandments found in the biblical book of Exodus.

Pause for a moment and think of this: If enough people banded together to think that murder is morally acceptable, then it could potentially change laws related to murder. In a very complex process, this then would (theoretically) lead to a shift in morality and change in laws related to what once was deemed immoral and irrational. Just look at the Prohibition Era that we mentioned in an earlier chapter. In a fight for the Eighteenth Amendment, numerous amounts of people banded together to enact a law to make alcohol illegal, yet thirteen years later, enough people voted against it to "de-ratify it." Changes like this can easily take place. Thus, susceptibility to moral change is not as far-fetched as it may seem.

Ideological Shifts

The study of criminology and criminological theory will continue to be interdisciplinary. Little may change from the modern stance unless a significant ideological shift occurs. Crimes such as assisted suicide, spousal abuse, or elder abuse may undergo a fundamental modification and become misdemeanors instead of felonies, just as abortion was redefined from a criminal act to routine medical procedure. Fundamentals play a large role in ideological shifts, and I would like to think that if enough people banded together, and listened to their moral conscience, criminology would hearken back to its classical and neoclassical roots. Modern culture has adopted much less stringent punishments, and the rampant crime and overcrowding of local jails and federal institutions should serve as a call for change. "While the heyday of the classical school was more than 200 years ago, this does not mean that its ideas are antiquated."[4] If society as a whole would reconsider the Enlightenment period, and potentially the work of Friedrich Nietzsche, whose *On the Genealogy of Morals* suggested a moral

---

4. Ranasinghe, "Friedrich Nietzsche, *On the Genealogy of Morals*," 75.

CONCLUSION

driving force for criminal behavior, the justice system and prisons would arguably be in a much better state. While Nietzsche didn't exactly view that force as positive, its key tenets returned to the stances of Bentham and Beccaria regarding morality, choice (pain versus pleasure), and punishment.

THE BIBLICAL BASIS

I heard a quote once, whose source I am at a loss for, but it basically said, *Salvation was in the heart of God before sin was ever in the hand of man.* And it really struck a chord. In the end, does religion *really* play a role in how law enforcement officers deal with offenders on the daily? Most likely not. It does, however, serve to give both the officer and the offender a chance to examine each individual case and realize that only the offender is responsible for their actions in the crimes they have chosen to commit. As much as I personally hate to make the statement "everything is a choice," crime comes down to making a choice to do the right thing or do the wrong thing. It is a choice to follow the moral code, or not to. Simple as that.

Scripture speaks often about morality and immorality. It has been said that Scripture takes an overly pacifistic tone, especially in the New Testament as it advocates a consistent witness against violence and calls upon the community to accept suffering as Christ accepted suffering.[5] Yet it also often speaks about giving due regard to lawful authorities (whether divine, Christ, or human, law enforcement), like the following passages demonstrate. The following also serve to demonstrate that choices and morality are bound to one another:

> And he said, "What comes out of a person is what defiles him. For from within, out of the heart of man, come evil thoughts, sexual immorality, theft, murder, adultery, coveting, wickedness, deceit, sensuality, envy, slander, pride, foolishness. All these evil things come from within, and they defile a person." (Mark 7:20–23)

5. Hays, *Moral Vision of the New Testament*, 332.

Or do you not know that the unrighteous will not inherit the kingdom of God? Do not be deceived: neither the sexually immoral, nor idolaters, nor adulterers, nor men who practice homosexuality, nor thieves, nor the greedy, nor drunkards, nor revilers, nor swindlers will inherit the kingdom of God. And such were some of you. But you were washed, you were sanctified, you were justified in the name of the Lord Jesus Christ and by the Spirit of our God. (1 Cor 6:9–11)

Let every person be subject to the governing authorities. For there is no authority except from God, and those that exist have been instituted by God. Therefore, whoever resists the authorities resists what God has appointed, and those who resist will incur judgment. For rulers are not a terror to good conduct, but to bad. Would you have no fear of the one who is in authority? Then do what is good, and you will receive his approval, for he is God's servant for your good. But if you do wrong, be afraid, for he does not bear the sword in vain. For he is the servant of God, an avenger who carries out God's wrath on the wrongdoer. Therefore, one must be in subjection, not only to avoid God's wrath but also for the sake of conscience. (Rom 13:1–7)

For this reason God gave them up to dishonorable passions. For their women exchanged natural relations for those that are contrary to nature; and the men likewise gave up natural relations with women and were consumed with passion for one another, men committing shameless acts with men and receiving in themselves the due penalty for their error. And since they did not see fit to acknowledge God, God gave them up to a debased mind to do what ought not to be done. They were filled with all manner of unrighteousness, evil, covetousness, malice. They are full of envy, murder, strife, deceit, maliciousness. They are gossips, slanderers, haters of God, insolent, haughty, boastful, inventors of evil, disobedient to parents. (Rom 1:26–32)

This lapse in moral aptitude, lapse in critical thinking in the heat of the moment, can only be chalked up to choice. It is not anyone else's fault that you *chose* to commit a crime. You may *feel* like it was someone who made you do it. But that won't ever be the case. "Often it can be easier, and more comforting, to allocate blame than to investigate the true causes of a bad event. The act of blaming allows us to separate the good from the bad, leaving us on the side of the good."[6] This, in and of itself, is a direct result of sinfulness, temptation, and greed.

God has endowed each and every individual with a moral code and moral character that have been evident from the very beginning of creation. The quote above only serves to further this point: God *knew* everything from creation. He *knew* that his people would rebel and sin and get themselves into some hot water . . . on more than one occasion. *He knew*. And he still made a way for us to be delivered from it.

THE ETHICAL BASIS

There is a God who has revealed himself to us. This is the basis for knowledge and understanding the true world around us. A philosophy of ethics, morality, science, and everything in between finds its basis in the queen of sciences—theology. Worldview matters, even when it comes to criminological studies, as theories are rooted in them, from Christianity to atheism, from redemptive strategies to strict adherence to a penal code. Worldview is the framework from which every research strategy flows, including the basis for the oft overlooked "redemptive criminology." It can be said, then, that morality is undoubtedly connected to origins (from where worldview is derived) because beliefs have consequences. If there is no God, then who owns us? Who sets the rules? Thus, we begin with a biblical standpoint, a worldview, which comprises the following six key tenets listed in the section below. The tenets set the stage from where all ethics and morals flow according to

---

6. Dingwall and Hillier, *Blamestorming*, 166.

a *Christian ethic*. Other world religions have similar conceptual ideologies concerning worldview and base their views of morality off the foundational elements espoused in each of the following tenets, thus the need to cover the following in a biblical worldview.

Philosophy and Worldviews: A Biblical Perspective

At some point in an individual's life they question their existence, the reason why they are here, and raise ethical questions regarding life events. So, how do we understand these in-depth questions? How do we answer them to reach a logical conclusion? Ethical questions such as "Can we be good without God?" are answered with the axiological argument. The objectivity of moral values is seen as either relative or absolute. To the relativist (non-Christian) morality is subjective and non-binding, thus moral actions do not exist; and even if they did, we wouldn't really know what they are. To the absolutist, morals are fixed—there are standards that are for all people (such as the Ten Commandments; Exod 20:1–17) that set the standard for what is right and what is wrong. These absolute standards indicate a God because the morals are firmly rooted in God. God's nature is the absolute standard on which all actions and decisions are measured.[7]

If our morals are based on the nature of the Christian God, then wouldn't it logically be possible that time and space are also connected to a divine being? Isaac Newton, a Bible-believing scientist, noted that time and space are absolute. "They are absolute in the sense that they are unique. There is one universal time in which all events come to pass with determinate duration and in a determinate sequence and one, universal space in which all physical objects exist with determinate shapes and in determinate arrangement."[8] Thus, things remain similar and immovable since change requires something that transcends the power of

---

7. Moreland and Craig, *Philosophical Foundations for a Christian Worldview*, 490–91.

8. Moreland and Craig, *Philosophical Foundations for a Christian Worldview*, 370.

humans—they only become immovable through the power of God himself. Such passages as Ps 8:3–4 and Isa 40:26 suggest that our world and everything in it has its origin in the Christian God. Thus, a proper Christian worldview makes sense of who we are, how we are to act, and who our judge is.

Creation tells us that there is a God who created and designed everything and who created by his spoken word. This revelation of speaking everything into existence has linguistic underpinnings that reach to all of reality from the laws of nature to genetics. The nature of linguistic underpinnings implies intelligence and a mind that is non-material.[9] The Scriptures themselves are God revealing himself to us, and he continues to speak through his word today. God's self-revelation to mankind then becomes the basis for doing modern science, that is, for understanding the world around us. God's word reveals to us what he did, and how he did it, as he is the only eyewitness to all the events laid out in Scripture. We even see evidence that he created recently, evidence of design (common design *not* descent) through genomic blueprints, creation of non-material information, etc. Thus, we build a framework around the Creator and his creation for understanding the world around us and how we should interact with it. This has major implications in the moral realm, especially as it relates to information and decision-making in the realm of criminological behavior.

The fall reveals that something happened to the very good creation through the sin of man. The nature of man's sin brought death and suffering into creation, which was not originally part of his creation (*tov meod*). You could not have two more diametrically opposed views of death between worldviews. In a secular worldview, death has always been there (Carl Sagan said death and time were the foundation of evolutionary processes; thus death was an integral part of bringing about life in his view[10]). In the biblical worldview, man's sin is responsible for bringing about death. Death entered the world into God's good creation as a result of

---

9. Baumgardner and Lyon, "Linguistic Argument for God's Existence," 771–86.

10. Sagan, *Cosmos*.

sin, there is no other way; it's a statistical fact that every one out of one thing dies! God gave dominion over creation to man, which man's sin impacted at the fall. Sin marred the entire landscape of the earth (the world that then existed perished); sin thus ushered in death, faulty perceptions, crime, etc.

The flood was God's judgment on the wickedness of the world, thus doing away with all of the things he created. What we see today is the result of catastrophic processes due to man's sin. In other words, God once destroyed the earth because of lies, deceit, crime, and other lewd acts. Who's to say he won't "purify" it again because of these things, just in a different manner (2 Pet 3)?

Babel. How can one explain the origin of the nations and the separation of gene pools if we don't understand Babel? Sin marred the relevance of God to man, who ultimately desired to be higher than God (stemming from the garden of Eden). As languages were confused, and people groups moved into other parts of the world, the separation of gene pools can be determined if we understand Babel correctly. This isolation of gene pools, which developed into distinct cultures, is explained in Gen 10–11. However, even though languages were confused at Babel, the moral conscience (as mentioned in a previous chapter) is spoken so that all may understand its tenets. Thus, there is no excuse.

Christ and the cross are essential elements in the biblical worldview. God created man in his image, according to his likeness. God directly breathed life into the nostrils of Adam; he (Adam) was not a descendant of an animal of some sort. In the secular worldview, man is simply an animal who is a product of millions of years and natural selection and would have no moral consciousness, thus paving a way for a life of crime. In a biblical worldview, humans are the crown of creation; we are unique, as we have been given dominion over the earth (true definition of "creation care" or "environmentalism"). The Bible thus has now provided the framework for earth history and the origin of man. Christ steps into his creation as a descendant of Adam (clothed in humanity, virgin born). He bore the sins of mankind for the descendants of Adam. The Bible makes it clear that Christ only died for the descendants of Adam and that he would only do that *once*.

The consummation of Christ is relevant for the future hope that we have. Christ will return again and redeem those who believe in him. The future of the universe in the secular worldview is heat death, spiraling toward complete non-existence. In a biblical worldview, this fallen world will be done away with and all things will be made new—Eden restored with the Groom and his bride as expressed in Revelation. The earth is robust, yet we are to be good stewards of the earth and utilize its resources for our good. Only with the future coming of Christ does one find hope.

These ideals thus form the framework in which we understand the world around us. When we begin with Scripture, we recognize what God has revealed to us and we are able to develop a system of ethics based on God's revelation to mankind. There is certainly a God who speaks through genetic language to the laws of nature. God upholds the laws of nature itself by the word of his power. He offers a future restoration of the *tov meod* where there was no death or suffering. The moral laws written on the hearts of man are given by the Law Giver, just like the laws of nature. These immaterial things can only be given by something that is material, that is God. You cannot explain the immaterial through materialistic explanations. You cannot explain the origin of immaterial entities through materialistic mechanism. But you can, and must, explain the natural world as a result of the supernatural.

Ethics then is born out of this biblical worldview that is revealed to all mankind in Scripture. How do we deal with criminals who supposed that their genes made them do it? How do we deal with criminals who take no responsibility for the acts they've committed? From where do they derive their morals? Are their morals diametrically opposed to those of a biblical worldview? These questions hit at the heart of many people's understanding of ethics.

Ethics and morality are part and parcel of establishing a redemptive criminological strategy. Rehabilitation processes rest solely on the instillment of biblical ethics during the criminological process. We established that oftentimes the humanity of both

AN INCONVENIENT TRUTH

criminals and law enforcement is overshadowed by the crimes themselves, and we fail to recognize that no matter which side one looks at, both the criminal and the law enforcement officer are fallible human beings just like anyone else. There is never an acceptable time to fabricate or falsify evidence or claims, and there should be judiciary repercussions to deter these acts of fraud. Acceptable punishments should be meted out in light of the moral code that is embedded in the conscience of human beings, and just as punishments are dealt out, it should be incumbent upon those who enforce those laws to act in moral and ethical ways. While morality does not necessarily coincide directly with *every* law, it is a major contributor to it.[11] And it can even be said that many laws are "informed by, and even created by, morality."[12] Thus this is the basis for establishing the personal culpability in the choices we make to do right or do wrong.

WHY IT MATTERS IN THE END

You might be asking yourself *why* any of this matters—the worldviews, the ethics, the science, the morals . . . and, at this point, I hope you have an inkling as to why it should be at the forefront of your mind, or at the very least should be something you mull over. Our worldviews establish a basis for our understanding of our world, morality, good and evil, and everything in between. The Creator has endowed each and every individual with a moral compass to guide them in their decisions for their lives; that's the beauty of free will. What we do, as individuals, with that free will determines the outcomes of our lives—both in positive and negative lights.

Throughout history, object lessons in crime and punishment have been recorded and enacted. One of the biggest spectacles was that of the crucifixion. The public shaming and dehumanization of criminals in the Roman period were surefire ways of warning

---

11. Hayes, Carpenter, and Dwyer, *Sex, Crime and Morality*, 5.
12. Hayes, Carpenter, and Dwyer, *Sex, Crime and Morality*, 5.

CONCLUSION

other criminals about the consequences of their actions. Deterring others who sought to be insubordinate and taking their power away from them was the ultimate goal through these public spectacles. And that is just what they were: a public spectacle. Crucifixions were public events, instruments of punishment for the most despised people in society,[13] yet Christ was crucified and was blameless in his actions. He took on the shame, guilt, and agony of a painful death, all for what? To make our slates clean. To make a way for us to him. For atonement of our sins. He offered himself as a sacrifice on our behalf, heaping upon himself the totality of sin and personal culpability so that we may be made whole again.

---

13. Cone, *Cross and the Lynching Tree*, 161.

Bibliography

Allison, Gregg R. *Historical Theology*. Grand Rapids, MI: Zondervan, 2011.
Anderson, George, and Joseph Oppong. "Wife Battery: A Divine Command from the Garden of Eden or a Gene Disorder in Men? Ethical Perspectives." *Journal of Philosophy, Culture, and Religion* 42 (2019) 16–22.
Aniol, Scott. "Practice Makes Perfect: Corporate Worship and the Formation of Spiritual Virtue." *Journal of Spiritual Formation and Soul Care* 10.1 (2017) 93–104.
Aristotle. *Nicomachean Ethics*. Translated by Terrence Irwin. Indianapolis: Hackett, 1985.
Baker, Brenda J. "Contributions of Biological Anthropology to the Understanding of Ancient Egyptian and Nubian Societies." In *Anthropology and Egyptology: A Developing Dialogue*, edited by Judith Lustig, 106–16. Sheffield: Sheffield Academic, 1997.
Bassler, Jouette M. "Cain and Abel in the Palestinian Targums." *Journal for the Study of Judaism* 17 (1986) 56–64.
Bauerschmidt, Frederick Christian. "Ethics and the Triune God." In *The Routledge Companion to Christian Ethics*, edited by D. Stephen Long and Rebekah L. Miles, 6–17. London: Routledge, 2023.
Baumgardner, John R., and Jeremy D. Lyon. "A Linguistic Argument for God's Existence." *Journal of the Evangelical Theological Society* 58.4 (2015) 771–86.
Beccaria, Cesare. *Essay on Crimes and Punishments*. Livorno, Italy: Tipografia Coltellini, 1764. https://oll.libertyfund.org/titles/voltaire-an-essay-on-crimes-and-punishments.
Bentham, Jeremy. *An Introduction to the Principles of Morals and Legislation*. Oxford: Clarendon, 1907.

BIBLIOGRAPHY

Bloom, Paul. "Religion, Morality, Evolution." *Annual Review of Psychology* 63 (2012) 179–99.

Bonhoeffer, Dietrich. *Ethics*. New York: Macmillan, 1955.

Bosworth, Mary, and Carolyn Hoyle, eds. *What Is Criminology?* Oxford: Oxford University Press, 2011.

Britton, Dana M., Shannon K. Jacobsen, and Grace Howard. *The Gender of Crime*. 2nd ed. London: Rowman & Littlefield, 2018.

Brooks, Beatrice Allard. *A Contribution to the Study of the Moral Practices of Certain Social Groups in Ancient Mesopotamia*. Leipzig: W. Drugulin, 1921.

Burke, Roger Hopkins. *Contemporary Criminological Theory: Crime and Criminal Behaviour in the Age of Moral Uncertainty*. London: Routledge, 2020.

Burnside, Jonathan P. *The Signs of Sin: Seriousness of Offence in Biblical Law*. JSOTSupp 364. Sheffield: Sheffield Academic, 2003.

Byron, John. *Cain and Abel in Text and Tradition: Jewish and Christian Interpretations of the First Sibling Rivalry*. Leiden: Brill, 2011.

Cohen, A. B., and Michael E. W. Varnum. "Beyond East vs. West: Social Class, Region, and Religion as Forms of Culture." *Current Opinion in Psychology* 8 (2016) 5–9. https://doi.org/10.1016/j.copsyc.2015.09.006.

Cone, James. *The Cross and the Lynching Tree*. Maryknoll, NY: Orbis, 2011.

Daughtry, Will. "Reward for Missing 12-Year-Old Maria Gomez-Perez Increases to $50,000." *AccessWDUN*, June 19, 2024. https://accesswdun.com/article/2024/6/1248714/reward-for-missing-12-year-old-maria-gomez-perez-increases-to-50000.

Davies, Eryl W. "The Moral Vision of the Hebrew Bible: An Examination of Some Methodological Issues." In *Key Approaches to Biblical Ethics: An Interdisciplinary Dialogue*, edited by Volker Rabens et al., 154–70. Biblical Interpretation Series 189. Leiden: Brill, 2021.

Dingwall, Gavin, and Tom Hillier. *Blamestorming, Blamemongers, and Scapegoats: Allocating Blame in the Criminal Justice Process*. Bristol: Bristol University Press, 2015.

Dooley, Brendan D., and Michael Rocque. "Criminology's Future Is in Its Past." *Journal of Criminal Justice* 85 (Mar.–Apr. 2023). https://doi.org/10.1016/j.jcrimjus.2023.102043.

Durrant, Russil, and Zoe Poppelwell. *Religion, Crime and Punishment: An Evolutionary Perspective*. Cham, Switzerland: Palgrave Macmillan, 2017.

Dutelle, Aric W., and Randy S. Taylor. *Ethics for the Public Service Professional*. 2nd ed. London: Taylor & Francis, 2018.

Ellwood, Charles A. "Lombroso's Theory of Crime." *Journal of the American Institute of Criminal Law and Criminology* 2.5 (Jan. 1912) 716–23.

Enyioko, Newman. "Security Constitution: Issues to Consider in Crime and Punishment Following the Biblical Perspective." SSRN, Dec. 20, 2019. http://dx.doi.org/10.2139/ssrn.3507357.

Erikson, Kai. *Wayward Puritans: A Study in the Sociology of Deviance*. New York: Wiley, 1966.

BIBLIOGRAPHY

Felson, Marcus. *Crime and Everyday Life*. 2nd ed. Thousand Oaks, CA: Pine Forge, 1998.

Filangieri, Gaetano. *Ciencia de la legislación*. Translated by Juan Rivera. Madrid: Imprenta de D. Fermín Villalpando, 1821.

———. *Ciencia de la legislación*. 3rd ed. Traducción de Jaime Rubio. Madrid: Imprenta de Núñez, 1822.

Fingert, Tyler. "Maria Gomez-Perez Found Safe in Ohio, Guatemalan National Arrested." *Fox5 Atlanta*, July 26, 2024. https://www.fox5atlanta.com/news/maria-gomez-perez-found-safe-search-missing-12-year-old-ends-after-57-days.amp.

Frymer-Kensky, Tikva. "Israel." In *A History of Ancient Near Eastern Law*, edited by Raymond Westbrook, 975–1046. Leiden: Brill, 2003. https://doi.org/10.1163/9789047402091_028.

Gabbidon, Shaun L. "W.E.B. DuBois on Crime: Rethinking the Beginnings of American Criminology." *The Criminologist* 23.6 (Nov./Dec. 1998) 1–3.

Garfinkel, Harold. "Conditions of Successful Degradation Ceremonies." *American Journal of Sociology* 61.5 (1956) 420–24.

Gold, Azgad, and Paul S. Applebaum. "The Inclination to Evil and the Punishment of Crime—From the Bible to Behavioral Genetics." *Israel Journal of Psychiatry and Related Sciences* 51.3 (2014) 162–68.

Graham, Jesse, and Jonathan Haidt. "Beyond Beliefs: Religions Bind Individuals into Moral Communities." *Personality and Social Psychology Review* 14 (2010) 140–50. doi.org/10.1177/1088868309353415.

Green, Stuart P. *Lying, Cheating, and Stealing: A Moral Theory of White-Collar Crime*. Oxford: Oxford University Press, 2006.

Greenawalt, Kent. "Legal Enforcement of Morality." *Journal of Criminal Law and Criminology* 85.3 (Winter 1995) 710–25.

Griffith, Lee. *The Fall of the Prison: Biblical Perspectives on Prison Abolition*. Grand Rapids, MI: Eerdmans, 1993.

Halbwachs, Maurice. *La théorie de l'homme moyen: Essai sur Quetelet et la statistique morale* [*The Theory of the Average Man: Essay on Quetelet and Moral Statistics*]. Paris: Alcan, 1913.

Hart, H. L. A. *The Concept of Law*. 3rd ed. Oxford: Oxford University Press, 2012.

Harvey, Warren Zev. "Four Jewish Visions of the Garden of Eden." *Religions* 14.2 (2023) 221–32.

Hayes, Sharon, Belinda J. Carpenter, and Angela Dwyer. *Sex, Crime and Morality*. London: Routledge, 2012.

Hays, Richard B. *The Moral Vision of the New Testament: Community, Cross, New Creation; A Contemporary Introduction to New Testament Ethics*. New York: T&T Clark, 1997.

Herbert, Steve. "Morality in Law Enforcement: Chasing 'Bad Guys' with the Los Angeles Police Department." *Law and Society Review* 30.4 (1996) 799–818.

Hiers, Richard H. *Justice and Compassion in Biblical Law*. New York: Continuum, 2009.

BIBLIOGRAPHY

Hill, Mark. "Introduction." In *Christianity and Criminal Law*, edited by Mark Hill et al., 1–10. London: Routledge, 2020.

Hitchens, Christopher. *God Is Not Great: How Religion Poisons Everything*. New York: Allen & Unwin, 2007.

Hofweber, Thomas. "Logic and Ontology." *The Stanford Encyclopedia of Philosophy* (summer 2023 ed.), edited by Edward N. Zalta and Uri Nodelman. https://plato.stanford.edu/archives/sum2023/entries/logic-ontology/.

International Association of Chiefs of Police. "The Oath of Honor." https://www.theiacp.org/sites/default/files/2021-01/246910_IACP_Oath_of_Honor_11x8.5_p1%20%281%29.pdf.

Isaac, Monica L. "For Such a Time as This: A Social and Cultural Texture of Esther 4:1–17." *Journal of Biblical Perspectives in Leadership* 10.1 (Fall 2020) 56–65.

Kane, Robert. *The Significance of Free Will*. Oxford: Oxford University Press, 1998.

Laub, John H. "Life Course of Criminology in the United States: The American Society of Criminology Presidential Address." *Criminology* 42.1 (2004) 1–25.

Lindholm, Phil. "Judaism in the Context of Western Ethical Plurality." *Voices from the University: The Legacy of the Hebrew Bible*, edited by Heidi Szpek, 299–310. Lincoln, NE: iUniverse, 2002.

Maimonides, Moses. *The Guide of the Perplexed*. Translated by Shlomo Pines. Edited by Shlomo Pines and Leo Strauss. Chicago: University of Chicago Press, 1963.

Maine, Henry Sumner. *Ancient Law: Its Connection with the Early History of Society and Its Relation to Modern Ideas*. Boston: Beacon, 1963.

Marshall, Christopher D. *Beyond Retribution: A New Testament Vision for Justice, Crime, and Punishment*. Grand Rapids, MI: Eerdmans, 2001.

Masferrer, Aniceto. "The Role of Nature in the Secularization of Criminal Law in Europe (17th–19th Centuries)." In *Criminal Law and Morality in the Age of Consent: Interdisciplinary Perspectives*, edited by Aniceto Masferrer, 97–144. Cham, Switzerland: Springer, 2020.

McBride, Jennifer M., and Thomas Fabisiak. "Bonhoeffer's Critique of Morality: A Theological Resource for Dismantling Mass Incarceration." In *Dietrich Bonhoeffer: Theology and Political Resistance*, edited by Lori Brandt Hale and W. David Hall, 89–110. Lanham, MD: Lexington, 2020.

McNamara, Martin, and Paul V. M. Flesher. "Targum." *Oxford Bibliographies*, last updated Sept. 29, 2014. doi.org/10.1093/OBO/9780195393361-0187.

Merriam Webster Dictionary. "Ontology." https://www.merriam-webster.com/dictionary/ontology.

Moberly, Walter. *The Ethics of Punishment*. London: Faber & Faber, 1968.

Moreland, J. P. "Science, Miracles, Agency Theory, and The God-of-the-Gaps." In *In Defense of Miracles: A Comprehensive Case for God's Action in History*, edited by R. Douglas Geivett and Gary R. Habermas, 132–48. Downers Grove, IL: IVP Academic, 1997.

BIBLIOGRAPHY

Moreland, J. P., and William Lane Craig. *Philosophical Foundations for a Christian Worldview*. Downers Grove, IL: InterVarsity, 2003.
Müller-Wollermann, Renate. "Crime and Punishment in Pharaonic Egypt." *Near Eastern Archaeology* 78.4 (Dec. 2015) 228–35.
Nahmanides, Moses [Ramban]. *Perush ha-Torah*. Edited by Chaim Dov Chavel. Jerusalem: Mosad Harav Kook, 1962.
Niebuhr, Reinhold. *The Children of Light and the Children of Darkness*. New York: Scribner's, 1949.
———. *An Interpretation of Christian Ethics*. Louisville, KY: Westminster John Knox, 2021.
Nietzsche, Friedrich. *On the Genealogy of Morals: A Polemic*. Translated by Douglas Smith. Oxford: Oxford University Press, 2009.
Normore, Anthony H., and Brian D. Fitch. *Leadership in Education, Corrections, and Law Enforcement: A Commitment to Ethics, Equity, and Excellence*. Bingley, England: Emerald Group, 2011.
Oettli, Samuel. *Das Gesetz Hammurabis und die Thora Israels. Eine religions- und rechtsgeschichtliche Parallele*. Leipzig, 1903. Repr., Nabu, 2012.
Olweus, D. "Testosterone and Adrenaline: Aggressive and Antisocial Behaviour in Normal Adolescent Males." In *The Causes of Crime: New Biological Approaches*, edited by S. A. Mednick et al., 263–82. Cambridge: Cambridge University Press, 1987.
Oshima, T. M. "Morality and the Minds of the Gods: Divine Knowledge and Human Ignorance in Mesopotamian Prayers and Didactic Literature." *Hebrew Bible and Ancient Israel* 6.4 (2017) 386–430.
Park, C. L., D. Edmondson, and A. Hale-Smith. "Why Religion? Meaning as Motivation." In *APA Handbook of Psychology, Religion, and Spirituality*, edited by K. I. Pargament, 1:157–71. Washington, DC: APA, 2013.
Paulson, Ronald. *Sin and Evil: Moral Values in Literature*. New Haven, CT: Yale University Press, 2007.
Peled, Ilan. "The Laws of Delict in the Hebrew Bible and Their Ancient Near Eastern Forerunners: Analysing and Comparing Social Attitudes to Crime." *Journal for Semitics* 27.2 (2018) 1–22.
Pointer, Lindsey. *The Restorative Justice Ritual*. London: Routledge, 2020.
Pollock, Joycelyn M. *Ethical Dilemmas and Decisions in Criminal Justice*. Belmont, CA: Wadsworth, 2007.
Prenzler, Tim. *Ethics and Accountability in Criminal Justice: Towards a Universal Standard*. Bowen Hills, QLD: Australian Academic, 2009.
Pycroft, Aaron, and Clemens Bartollas. *Redemptive Criminology*. Bristol: Bristol University Press, 2022.
Quetelet, Adolphe. *Du système social et des lois qui le régissent* [*On the Social System and the Laws That Govern It*]. Paris: Guillaumin, 1848.
Ranasinghe, Prashan. "Friedrich Nietzsche, *On the Genealogy of Morals* and Criminology." *Theoretical Criminology* 26.1 (Feb. 2022) 75–90.
Rawls, John. "The Justification of Civil Disobedience." In *Civil Disobedience*, edited by H. A. Bedau, 244–53. New York: Pegasus, 1969.

BIBLIOGRAPHY

Ritner, Robert K. *The Libyan Anarchy: Inscriptions from Egypt's Third Intermediate Period*. Atlanta: Society of Biblical Literature, 2009.

Roth, Martha T. *Law Collections from Mesopotamia and Asia Minor*. 2nd ed. Atlanta: Scholars Press, 1997.

Roth, Mitchel P. *An Eye for an Eye: A Global History of Crime and Punishment*. London: Reaktion, 2014.

Rush, Benjamin. *Medical Inquiries and Observations: Upon the Diseases of the Mind*. Philadelphia: Kimber and Richardson, 1812. web.english.upenn.edu/~cavitch/pdf-library/Rush_Diseases_of_the_Mind_1812_edition.pdf.

Ryrie, Charles C. "The Christian and Civil Disobedience." In *Readings in Christian Ethics, Volume 2: Issues and Applications*, edited by David K. Clark and Robert V. Rakestraw, 433–39. Grand Rapids, MI: Baker Academic, 1996.

Sabbatini, Renato M. E. "Phrenology: The History of Brain Localization." *Brain and Mind* 1 (Mar.–May 1997). cerebromente.org.br/n01/frenolog/frenologia.htm.

Sagan, Carl. *Cosmos*. New York: Ballantine, 1980.

Schmalleger, Frank. *Criminology Today: An Integrative Introduction*. 10th ed. New York: Pearson Education, 2021.

Sidgwick, H. *Outlines of the History of Ethics for English Readers*. 5th ed. London: Macmillan, 1902.

Sousa, William H., and George L. Kelling. "Of 'Broken Windows' Criminology and Criminal Justice." In *Police Innovation: Contrasting Perspectives*, edited by David Weisburd and Anthony A. Braga, 121–41. Cambridge: Cambridge University Press, 2006.

Stanberry, Jenn. "Western Jurisprudence: A Legacy of the Hebrew Bible." In *Voices from the University: The Legacy of the Hebrew Bible*, edited by Heidi Szpek, 311–28. Lincoln, NE: iUniverse, 2002.

Strawn, Brent A., ed. "Biblical Law." In *The Oxford Encyclopedia of the Bible and Law*. Oxford: Oxford University Press, 2015.

Tannenbaum, Frank. *Crime and the Community*. New York: Columbia University Press, 1938.

Varese, Federico. *Mafias on the Move: How Organized Crime Conquers New Territories*. Princeton, NJ: Princeton University Press, 2011.

Virkkunen, Matti. "Metabolic Dysfunctions Amongst Habitually Violent Offenders: Reactive Hypoglycaemia and Cholesterol Levels." In *The Causes of Crime: New Biological Approaches*, edited by S. A. Mednick et al., 292–311. Cambridge: Cambridge University Press, 1987.

Wall, Steven. *Enforcing Morality*. Cambridge: Cambridge University Press, 2023.

Weisburd, David. "The Law of Crime Concentration and the Criminology of Place." *Criminology* 53.2 (May 2015) 133–57.

Westbrook, Raymond. "Biblical and Cuneiform Law Codes." *Revue Biblique* 92.2 (1985) 247–64.

BIBLIOGRAPHY

———. "The Deposit Law of Exodus 22,6–12." *Zeitschrift für die alttestamentliche Wissenschaft* 106.3 (1994) 390–403. https://doi.org/10.1515/zatw.1994.106.3.390.

———. "Introduction: The Character of Ancient Near Eastern Law." In *A History of Ancient Near Eastern Law*, edited by Raymond Westbrook, 1–90. Leiden: Brill, 2003. https://doi.org/10.1163/9789047402091_002.

———. *Studies in Biblical and Cuneiform Law*. Paris: Gabalda, 1988.

———. "What Is the Covenant Code?" In *Theory and Method in Biblical and Cuneiform Law: Revision, Interpretation, and Development*, edited by Bernard M. Levinson, 15–36. Sheffield: Sheffield Academic Press, 1994.

Wiedemann, Felix. "Moses or Hammurabi? Law, Morality, and Modernity in Ancient Near Eastern Studies." In *Moses Among the Moderns: German Constructions of Biblical Law, 1750–1930*, 90–114. Leiden: Brill, 2024.

Wikström, Per-Olof H., and Robert J. Sampson, eds. *The Explanation of Crime: Context, Mechanisms, and Development*. Cambridge: Cambridge University Press, 2006.

Winright, Tobias. "Crucifixion, Torture, and Capital Punishment." In *The Routledge Companion to Christian Ethics*, edited by D. Stephen Long and Rebekah L. Miles, 260–74. London: Routledge, 2023.

Wood, Allen W. *Kant's Ethical Theory*. Cambridge: Cambridge University Press, 1999.

Zashin, Elliot M. *Civil Disobedience and Democracy*. New York: Free Press, 1972.

www.ingramcontent.com/pod-product-compliance
Lightning Source LLC
Chambersburg PA
CBHW071738090426
42738CB00011B/2525